Memoir of the Fens:
An Ely Education

Memoir of of the Fens:
An Ely Education

PAULINE TAMBLING

Copyright © 2026 Pauline Tambling

The moral right of the author has been asserted.

Apart from any fair dealing for the purposes of research or private study, or criticism or review, as permitted under the Copyright, Designs and Patents Act 1988, this publication may only be reproduced, stored or transmitted, in any form or by any means, with the prior permission in writing of the publishers, or in the case of reprographic reproduction in accordance with the terms of licences issued by the Copyright Licensing Agency. Enquiries concerning reproduction outside those terms should be sent to the publishers.

The manufacturer's authorised representative in the EU for product safety is Authorised Rep Compliance Ltd, 71 Lower Baggot Street, Dublin D02 P593 Ireland (www.arccompliance.com)

Troubador Publishing Ltd
Unit E2 Airfield Business Park,
Harrison Road, Market Harborough,
Leicestershire. LE16 7UL
Tel: 0116 2792299
Email: books@troubador.co.uk
Web: www.troubador.co.uk

ISBN 978-1-80634-338-6

British Library Cataloguing in Publication Data.
A catalogue record for this book is available from the British Library.

Printed and bound in Great Britain by 4edge Limited
Typeset in 10pt Adobe Garamond Pro by Troubador Publishing Ltd, Leicester, UK

To all the young people whose lives Pauline touched

Contents

	Preface: Jeremy Tambling	ix
	Introduction	xxiii
1	The History – the Isle of Ely: 'A far greater country'	1
	Ely's early history	3
	King Cnut's visits to the fens	6
	The abbeys and monasteries	8
	The early drainage projects	10
	Drainage under the Stuart Kings	12
	Impact of the drainage projects on local people	14
	Vermuyden's legacy	15
	Finishing the job	16
	The 1947 Floods	17
2	Education	18
3	My Mother's family	36
	The Peterborough to Ely railway line	39
	The railway developments of the 1840s	40
	Migration to the Fens in the late 1840s	41
	A childhood in the fens	44
4	My mother's family	46
	Whittlesea	53

| vii

	The Neals of Turves	56
	Stuntney, 1915	60
5	The Americans Arrive	61
	Black Horse Drove 1884	61
	Ely 1960	63
	Childhood	68
	The Americans	71
6	Rhoda Francis Clements	77
	Burnt Fen 1801	77
	Littleport May 1816	79
	Ely June 1816	84
	Prickwillow 1820	87
	Widowed	91
	Soham 1866	91
7	The Clements	93
	Hope Brothers Shirt and Collar Factory	99
	The Dorlings	101
8	Rachel Clements and her family	104
	Ely, 1968	104
	Sarah Clements: Billy's Mother	110
9	Maria Clements and Lambeth	114
	North Lambeth 1850s	118
	The Woosters	121
	Beckett Street, Camberwell 1870s	126
	Camberwell, 1880s	129
	Ely 1906	134
10	Ely High School for Girls – and more clues	136
	Coda and Acknowledgements (Jeremy Tambling)	144
	Bibliography	162

Preface:

Jeremy Tambling

I want to introduce this memoir by quoting an obituary for my wife, who died on December 1 2023; it appeared in the *Guardian* 'Other Lives' on February 13 2024, written by Sally Bacon:

> *My friend and colleague Pauline Tambling, who has died of cancer aged 68, played a huge role in the arts education world for four decades. She was one of very few people to work successfully across arts education, employment, and policy development at a national level, for organisations including the Royal Opera House, then Arts Council of England, and the National Skills Academy.*
>
> *Having started out as a teacher, in 1983 Pauline became the first education officer for the Royal Opera (the ROH having recruited an education officer for the Royal Ballet the previous year), as a result of the recommendation in the 1982 Gulbenkian Foundation Arts in Schools report that cultural organisations create education posts. The "Write an Opera" scheme she created in 1985 is still going,*

as is the European network of opera education departments that she co-founded.

Born in Ely, Cambridgeshire, Pauline was the daughter of Annie (née Butcher), a factory worker, cleaner and cook, and Bill Dorling, a labourer and hospital porter. After Ely high school for girls, she gained her teaching certificate at Stockwell College, Bromley, south London, in 1973. Her first job was as a religious studies teacher at a comprehensive school in Brent, in north-west London. She then taught at a primary school in rural Essex, before joining the Royal Opera.

In 1997 Pauline was made Director of Education and Training at the Arts Council of England, rising to an Executive Director position. There she was the prime mover behind several major national initiatives including Creative Partnerships (2002-2011), which aimed to engage young people in schools with creative practitioners, and the charity Youth Music.

She became chief operating officer of Creative & Cultural Skills (CCSkills) in 2007, soon becoming joint chief executive and managing director of the National Skills Academy, a national network of further education colleges working with the creative industries. In 2013 Pauline became chief executive of CCSkills, where she was involved in creating High House Production Park, a regeneration project in Thurrock, Essex. Here she was responsible for the building of the Backstage Centre, a training and rehearsal space co-located with ROH workshops.

Pauline had lived with cancer since 2017. After retiring from CCSkills the following year she continued to remain active in the education and arts sector, in many trustee and chair roles.

Preface: Jeremy Tambling

> *Her career came full circle when she revisited the 1982 Arts in Schools report. Her 2023 report, The Arts in Schools: Foundations for the Future, which she and I wrote together, calls for arts subjects to be central to a rethink of England's state education system.*
>
> *Pauline was an unassuming powerhouse – a dynamo of ideas and great fun. A fabulous collaborator and strategist, she was always generous with her time and superb at navigating complexity to make positive things happen which would go on to have a lasting impact. She was appointed CBE in 2014.*
>
> *In 1976 Pauline married Jeremy Tambling, an English lecturer and latterly professor of literature. He survives her, as do their children, Kirsten and Felix, and four grandchildren, Frances, Emil, and Sidonie, and Marcela.*

My thanks go to Sally Bacon for writing that. Sally was one of those who took part in a memorial for Pauline on January 23, 2024, and I give her speech in full at the end of the book. The memorial event took place at the Round House, where Pauline had been an advisor: they named a room after her in Roundhouse Works. The other speakers were Marcus Davey, the Chief Executive and Artistic Director of the Roundhouse, and Peter Renshaw, who had been Director, Performance and Communication Skills Project, Guildhall School of Music & Drama. The appointment was supported by the Gulbenkian Foundation, and Alex Beard, the Chief Executive Officer of the Royal Opera House (henceforth ROH). Then came Sally Bacon, and Kate Castle, who worked at the ROH as its first Ballet Education Officer, and who was a close and dear friend. I give her speech at the end. The last speaker was Elizabeth Hosker, a lovely family friend and musician, who played, solo, in memory of Pauline's music talents, Bach's Bourree

I and II from the 3rd cello suite, which she arranged for viola. She also created, for the event, a tape of the music that Pauline listened to most. Two hundred people were there, as a tribute to Pauline: there were many others who could not make it, such as Stephanie Hutchinson, who worked with Pauline at the Royal Opera House, after the education work had bedded into the institution, and Caroline Clarke (surname now Maxwell), who also worked there. (The burial, in a woodland setting, at Brinkley, had been more private, but there were women there, who had known Pauline from the age of four, Carol Easey (née Layton: their mothers were friends); and five, Rosemary Spalding (née Russell); and two from the age of eleven, Frances Hatch, and Elaine Oakey (née Lawrence).

Pauline had had a good, varied career, enjoying the Opera House – her favourite operas were *Rigoletto* and *La traviata*, and, decidedly, *Peter Grimes* (she enjoyed the Elijah Moshinsky production of that, which we saw with Robert Tear as Grimes), and she was a fervent Wagnerian. As an enthusiast for film, about which she was very knowledgeable, she also found the Andrei Tarkovsky production of *Boris Godunov* exceptional (it was typical of Pauline to go on noting little details of that production: Pauline loved detail). A book she authored, *Performing Arts in the Primary School* (Oxford: Blackwell 1990), and which was encouraged into being by the educationalist and headteacher Henry Pluckrose (1931-2011), who came to work at the education department at the Royal Opera House in 1986, discussed projects which she had worked on, and passed on valuable advice on the creative arts in schools. In September 1997, she devised a series for the BBC which was produced by Nel Romano, called *Top Score*, based around a production of Verdi's *Don Carlos* (another favourite of hers). She enjoyed working at the Arts Council of England, and in CC Skills, and in a sense outgrew the Opera House, becoming more fervently devoted to education for those who needed apprenticeships and needed to develop skills for that. Her ideal was developing apprenticeship schemes.

On the occasion of her getting the CBE in 2014, a celebration for her was held in the Linbury Studios at Covent Garden. I made a speech, which ran thus:

I'd like to begin with a thank you to those who have put this event together: Alex Beard and the Royal Opera House for giving the space, Catherine Large for organising it, and Alistair Renolds for being the curator. I've got the unusual job of trying to think objectively about what Pauline has done, and summarising it from my point of view, as having been married to her since 1976. Everyone here knows how much Pauline has done frontstage, and backstage, to achieve the CBE, and just how much she deserves it, but it's only me who knows how much that is only a part, and that there is a lot, backstage of the backstage centre to be talked about; in trying to sum it up in my head, I know I have missed many of the things she's done. Pauline is formidable in her range of abilities, but she is very quiet about them. But there is no mistaking how many things count for her in her life, and just how hard she has had to work.

I'd say Pauline has two interests which are inseparable for her: one is in the arts, and the other is in education. She was born in Ely, into a good old Labour family who did everything, and believed you should do everything, whose background was farming, and where if you didn't do whatever it was, no one else would do it for you. Pauline was brought up to do such small things as helping build a bungalow from scratch at weekends, which I think made absolutely inevitable building the Backstage Centre at Purfleet (in Essex) with its studios and offices and performance space, even when she had to fight for it, as I know she did. From her family she learned that the only way up and on is through education. She was expected, with virtually no discussion, to go into primary teaching, so she trained in religious studies, because it seemed a good idea at the time, but because there were no jobs then, and she had to take what she could, she went straight into one of the toughest comprehensive schools in Harrow (I don't mean *that* Harrow), where, by the end of the year, she was asked to become head of the Religious Studies department. Her favourite pupil took A level, with the police sitting behind him, to arrest him when he'd finished, for one of his many brushes with the law. But she didn't take the job further than one year, because she had already got married, and had moved to Colchester, and was looking for a job in schools there. After two temporary posts, she saw an advertisement for a teacher with special responsibility for music at a local, and deprived, primary school at Kirby Cross in Essex. I shall never forget her practising the Children's Suite by Debussy, which she was determined to make as her interview star turn, and by virtue of which playing she walked away with the job. That's how she got into music education; teaching and engaging in school performances, including a legendary *Wizard of Oz*, with a colleague, Maurice Anderson, where she provided the music all on her own. In the evenings she went off to do guitar lessons, and singing lessons, with a view to applying to become a deputy head, but then she saw the post for Education Officer at Covent Garden, a new venture, which the management had had to take on because Ken Livingstone in his then very good days, had threatened their funding if they didn't do some educational outreach. I do not think the management had any idea what they wanted, but all credit to them that they knew the person when they saw her. I'd already taken Pauline to ENO before, if I can mention that name here (the first opera she saw was *Carmen* in the late 1970s), but she'd never been near this particular sacred shrine. Nor had I. I raced to get the last tickets for whatever was on the night before the interview (it was *Don Pasquale*), and the next day, when they were wondering whether to appoint her, I am not sure why they needed to think about it, one of the committee members was heard to say, 'well she obviously knows the repertoire'. Pauline was in, and that started fourteen years of extraordinary achievement, which led to a senior post at the Arts Council which special responsibility for its creative and training programme, and doing everything besides, and then to where she is today, heading up Creative and Cultural Skills.

Pauline has never cut a corner, and she has always had a passionate vision for education at all levels, and I will also say for music, and all the creative arts. For a symbol of how Pauline stands for steady continuity and for renewal, and for promise, I'll give you those marvellous buildings at Purfleet, as a symbol of what Pauline has achieved. They combine the best of the seventeenth century in the farmhouse and orchard, and the stylish old layout, and the best of the modern, an intelligent building in every sense of that word, so they represent continuity, and growth, and they are built in the most improbable of all spaces, in Thurrock, a completely neglected part of Essex, which the politicians have only discovered since Pauline did (it was Labour, and Conservative, and UKIP). Pauline has made that a success, but I know she would say that's only because she has had a wonderful team behind her. And if she has such a team, and has made such a success, creating continuity in all she does, that is also because she has a sense of what people are worth, which is practical, and wonderful. (The Backstage Centre was located in High House Production Park, in Thurrock; this, thanks to Tony Hall's initative (he was then CEO of the ROH), also housed the ROH's painting scenery and prop production).

Pauline will never say it, but I can see that she has had to fight quite a few battles to get her vision appreciated past one or two myopic males who thought they should have the ideas and the credit. But her feminism, which used to take her to Greenham Common in the 1980s, has always been practical, as well as strategic. And if we are talking about battles, I know too of the bout she had with cancer eleven years back [2003], where she never surrendered the continuity of her day work throughout the most aggressive chemotherapy, and where it took a year for her to get back her wonderful appetite for good food. If we are talking about her diligence, I know how she has thought nothing of travelling all over the UK in the course of a week to speak to colleges or colleagues, or sort out some mess in a regional office, or to fund raise, or to give support. I know the genius she has for fund-raising, because I have seen her at it, writing bids and grant-proposals late into the night, and I can only wonder where she got these creative and cultural skills from: from an unfussy, understated and unsentimental country background where she was expected to be both the brains and to pitch in to every kind of work going, which has given her the taste for life and for passing on opportunities to others.

Her commitment goes with a very high standard when it comes to the arts, to theatre, to film, to music, to photography, all of which she keeps up with, and about all of which she has something to say. As one of those who from earliest childhood learned to work by brain and by hand, I can say she is a superb gardener, excellent at French and German, a cook of amazing versatility, speed and lack of fuss, cooking a rumbaba to die for if you're lucky, a mean talent at crochet-work, an intense reader, and a game traveller through South-east Asia, Europe, as a matter of course, and Latin America, so long as she is not pursued by adoring mosquitoes, who like all of us, appreciate what she stands for. And you will not be surprised to know she has just been gutting and rebuilding a new old house in Suffolk that she plans for weekends. And it all goes along with a strong sense of humour, and a readiness to take advice, and a sense of what matters in life, together with a huge tolerance for those who think differently. I haven't mentioned Kirsten and Felix, both now independent adults, but I know how much she has invested in them as children, and as making their way. But that's the thing about Pauline: you think something matters, and ought to be done, and then wonder what to do, and then find she thought about some time ago, and has done it already. She is a marvel, a miracle, without the solemnity which goes with being those things, and she's only now at the top of her game.

During the COVID epidemic, Pauline, who was very vulnerable to the virus, because of all the antibiotics she was on which had reduced her immune system to nothing, began to write her memoir. We were locked down in our little cottage in Woodbridge, Suffolk, and when we could, made journeys out to Ely and beyond, fifty miles away, to take photographs of the Cambridgeshire Fens, an area she had been brought up in, and which she felt had never been given any adequate representation, and which when it had been described, seemed to be very ignorant of what unique character it had and has. Cambridgeshire – apart, of course from Cambridge, though that is a dull town, redeemed only by the attractiveness of its colleges, and their architecture, remains a poor relation. It is not East Anglia, where both Norfolk and Suffolk have been so much written about, nor rural Essex, from which it is so different. To cross to Cambridgeshire from the gently rolling rises and falls of Suffolk low hills, and from a landscape which has a 'heritage' character to the flat unloveliness of the Fens, was always strange. What follows is that memoir which she wrote in those days; a memoir which is virtually and deliberately confined to describing her first eighteen years of life, and not at all her professional career. Hence she does not refer to me (she says 'we' when I am involved), nor her children, nor grandchildren (one more has arrived since her death: Marcela).

As she prodded into the details of her early life, she became more and more interested in the relations she barely knew, and of other lives which noone in her immediate family ever discussed, and might not even have been aware of. She had to follow whatever leads she could get, and was struck by how many different directions, nearly all unsuspected, they led her towards. She was struck by how the Fens had not proved to be a means of livelihood for many, how so many had moved away. The following is one of her notes:

Chapter X - Those that left

    Samuel, John and Sarah Clements to the USA
    Maria Clements – to South London
    Richard Clements to Eston (North Yorkshire) 1875
    Frederick Clements to Eston 1881
    Rhoda Clements to Eston 1891
    William Clements to Eston 1911
    James King (Mary Clements' son) to Keighley in Yorkshire
    John Nathaniel King (Mary Clements' son) to USA to join Mary Rhodes Clements
    Levi Francis (Rhoda Clements' brother) 1799-1870 – In 1861 his sons Jacob (1836-1926) and Fincham (1830-1918) to West Ham working on the new Bazalgette sewers.

The details of these names, which will obviously not mean much here, are filled in in what follows, but when the memoir is read through, to come back to those names will be interesting and perhaps enlightening. (If readers despair of sorting out all the names, that only repeats my puzzlement, and that of the protagonists themselves: Pauline's extended family were quite capable of confusing grandmothers, in almost Proustian fashion.) The names indicate how much unfulfilment was in those lives - and the same must apply today. Particularly what struck her, and strikes me on re-reading, is how few people managed to lift themselves out of poverty; how many ended in the workhouse; how many live ended prematurely. In writing up all the material she accumulated, Pauline was compelled to digress again and again; the memoir reads as an intersection of history and geography, and of her own childhood, as constructed by the past, and of the past as something which she researched with all the determination she had (and the lack of adequate tools to do so).

The Memoir was never completed; Pauline was always adding things, and wanting to develop things she had found, and discovered that none of her remaining relations knew the first thing about the names she had turned up; nor had they much interest in knowing about them. It all indicates what a strange thing families and extended families are: and there are many grim reminders of the hardship of rural and small town working-class lives, lives which could never quite ride the wave, but were always submerged by the unremitting character of poverty and lack of opportunity. There was just no romance in these lives, and the adjective which always seemed appropriate was 'flat'; the landscape was flat; there was a flatness about people's living and working conditions; there was a flatness required in the writing to depict the utter ordinariness of lives and occupations, and the unsentimentality required to live day by day. Pauline wanted to write about that, with no sense that her family were unique, or that these lives could not be replicated over and over again in other people's experience.

In this Memoir, the facts speak flatly and directly for

themselves. The lack of opportunity reminds me of Pauline's dedication to education, and to the need to give people opportunities: she fought that battle all her life, and it gave her her drive, which was ultimately defeated by returning cancer. She was always sensitive to the point that she did not have a degree, and that much of the time she was dealing with colleagues who had; it made her go for an MA at Bretton Hall, amongst her other achievements. There is one other point I would mention. English spoken at home was idiomatic and to the point, and though it produced some wonderful phrases, it never allowed her to 'take off', and she told me that she had bought a 'Teach Yourself' book for English language, and of only just passing 'O' Level English language. But Pauline took to French at her girls' grammar school with zest and accuracy, and all her life was immediately comfortable in conversational French, and loved France, too, where we spent so many holidays. I would go so far as to say she was happier in French than in English, and I think that is an amazing thought about what good education can do. Her A Level texts, which included Racine's *Andromache* and Moliere's *L'Ecole des femmes* and *Le Grand Meaulnes* and *La Porte Etroite* and *la Machine infernale* stayed with her as constant reference- points. Perhaps the objectivity required in French grammar, which at least in written form does not betray class, worked well for her. (But towards the end of hr life, she became very interested in Edouard Louis, and Didier Eribon, and Annie Ernaux: I am looking at her annotated French copies as I write.) The same point, without arguing whether music is a language, could be made about her devotion to classical music, which she took to 'O" Level, and could have taken much further, and about which she was always intelligently articulate. In a sense, this book is educational, not only because Pauline learned so much in writing it, but because she is passing on the histories of so many lives whose experiences, troubles, and struggles ought to be told, both to honour their memories, and to give a sense of the conditions of semi-rural life in the nineteenth and twentieth centuries.

Did Pauline love the Fens? Her reaction, every time we saw them, and travelled through them, was complex: the question what could be said that was positive about them and about Ely was always in her mind. But she wanted the Fens and Fen life to be described as they were for so many, and not to be romanticised.

I have acted as editor here, not changing anything, certainly not trying to resolve the questions of the previous paragraph! – but trying to synthesise the various and several versions of what she wrote, and remembering conversations I had with her about her book, I have tried, sometimes vainly, to organise the chapters, something she despaired of doing. I have not attempted to add anything at the end, and there is a fittingness in that: she never felt that she had completed her life: indeed she had applied for another post just weeks before receiving the last definitive cancer diagnosis which compelled her to stop her professional life, and until she died, to work only as an unpaid advisor. She would never have stopped voluntarily; her death was no rounding off of things, but an unwelcome intrusion to a life which had had so much in it which was flat, unpropitious, adversarial, and downright difficult, but where she succeeded so brilliantly.

Introduction

When I was a very small child in the late 1950s and early 1960s my mother told me that I would never be lost because I lived in Ely and Ely Cathedral was the tallest building for miles around and everywhere outside the 'city' was so flat that I would always be able to see the cathedral and get back home. I knew from a young age that Ely was a city even though it only had 10,000 inhabitants because of its cathedral. In fact Ely gained its city status in 1109.

Ely in the 1960s was a small place. Even as a child my friends and I could easily walk from the Royal Air Force hospital which edged Ely to the north and where my mother worked, to the railway station in the south, and from St John's Road in the west to Prickwillow Road in the east. Both ways were about two miles. Beyond the built-up area there were flat black fields of Cambridgeshire farmland all around edged by roads and dykes but no footpaths, and with few trees and no hedges. There were a lot of heavy farm vehicles on the roads and it was dangerous to walk beyond the town itself and there was little temptation to do so. From wherever we found ourselves there was no problem in aiming for the cathedral and then walking the length of the road from the centre of Ely to our house which was on the main A10

ELY CATHEDRAL SEEN FROM WADE'S FARM

towards Littleport, exactly half-way between the RAF hospital and the cathedral. Since then the population has doubled and the city has expanded filling the space between the place that I knew and a new by-pass and even newer ring-road that surrounds the town.

The cathedral was difficult to ignore because it dominated Ely in every way: all major events took place there including services for all the Christian festivals, Hospital Sunday (a traditional carnival fundraiser) and Armistice Day each November when as Girl Guides we marched alongside the other 'uniformed groups' and the men and women of the Royal British Legion to the cathedral for the service of remembrance and then on to Market Square where we would lay wreaths at a small war memorial set into the walls backing on to the cathedral grounds. Much later when at secondary school we played in concerts and carol services in the transept under Ely Cathedral's spectacular octagon tower. In 1973 there was a celebration for the thirteenth centenary of the monastery which had been founded in 673, pre-dating the abbey church which would later become the cathedral itself.

From the age of about seven my friends and I were free to go wherever we wanted in the evenings and school holidays. In the holidays we would often set off in the morning and return in the evening. Parents were working, and keys to our houses were left under flowerpots or on shelves in outside toilets or sheds so that we could get into the houses if we needed to, but we never did. There was no expectation of lunch when our parents were away, someone's mother would feed us, and there was no reason to stay at home alone. We would wander to playing fields, the cemetery, or into the town. In such a small place there was no way to slip under the radar because wherever we went we would be seen by someone our parents knew and they would report back on what we were doing. No one's parents organised activities for their children. I assumed this was normal but later learned that such freedoms were for the children from working-class homes. Middle-class children were more supervised.

On Saturday mornings we would play in the cathedral, joining free guided tours up to the top of the West Tower at 11 o'clock followed by a trip to a local café in Market Street where we would buy 'orange floaters': orange squash with a dollop of ice-cream served in a tall glass, eaten with a spoon. Sometimes we would walk round the floor maze under the cathedral's West Tower, or circle around the outside of the building mapping out the graves. In the summer holidays my friends and I would wander into Ely Park and down to the River Ouse, then much more separated from the town than now, and on Thursdays we would go to the cattle market and watch the auctioning of cows, pigs and sheep. The local farmers were there to sell their stock. After each auction the animals were pushed out of the auction ring with electrical prodders and into lorries taking them to the abattoir. The large animals were auctioned in the morning and afterwards we would go to another part of the live-stock market where small animals like rabbits and hens were sold. When we were older we would ride our bicycles into the surrounding Fen as far as Prickwillow or Littleport cycling on B roads and droves between the huge black fields where onions, carrots and sugar beet were grown. If our mothers took on seasonal farm work, which they often did, we would go too and help. One summer we earned twenty-one shillings (£1.05) each wringing onions. In our teens we all had Saturday jobs which spilled over into the holidays. At thirteen (1968) I worked as a shop assistant in Thornhill's Bakery, a local baker and confectioner based in Littleport with shops in Ely and Cambridge, and then moved on to be a shop assistant at Woolworth's which was in Fore Hill. As shop girls (there were never shop boys) we worked eight hours on a Saturday. In those days the store was made up of a number of units arranged as islands with a space in the middle for two shop assistants and the cash registers, then £sd, not 'new money' and the shop products were all around. Most of the units stocked the same products all year round but I worked on one that changed throughout the year: sometimes detergents, sometimes gardening equipment and plants, and in the run up to Christmas seasonal decorations. There were rotas for fifteen-minute tea and coffee breaks, and for a thirty minute lunch break. In 1970 Britain converted to decimal coinage and we High School Saturday girls were pulled in after school to hold the fort while the full-time staff were trained in the new system. [Pauline doesn't mention the considerable amount of waitressing she also did, sometimes with her mother – JT.]

This was in the 1960s when life was mostly uneventful in the area. There was minimal opportunity to leave Ely. There was a station with trains to Cambridge and London, and to King's Lynn and Norwich but no one I knew took the train anywhere. Ely had only one man who commuted to London at the time, a father of one of the girls in my class at grammar school. Buses went to the neighbouring villages of Littleport, Soham and Witchford but there was no reason to go to any of them. They were for villagers coming into Ely for the Thursday market or to visit family or friends.

There were occasional reminders that the world was not as safe as it seemed. Two boys went missing once and after some days of searching were found in the Roswell Pits, which were at the time disused clay pits but are now part of a large nature reserve. Children sometimes died: one I remember following an asthma attack, another having fallen down some stairs. There would often be stories in the local paper, the Ely Standard, of young drivers who, having recently passed their driving test but unused to the fenland roads which were dark, uneven and with deep dykes on both sides, died in accidents when their cars had ended up in ditches.

Talking to friends now I realise that what was happening in the rest of the UK failed to impact on our lives at all. Ely was sheltered from external changes. It was a particular and peculiar place in which to grow up. There was at the time little spoken about local history and when I left in the early 1970s I had little idea of Ely's history or of that of my family. In 2020 during the Covid pandemic I started to find out about my parents' families and about Ely.

My great-great grandparents, Rhoda and John Clements saw growth from nearly 4,000 when they married in 1801 to nearly 8,000 in 1862. A map from 1610 produced by John Speed shows that much of the centre of the city was already in place by the seventeenth century. The buildings surrounding the cathedral changed very little – although many historical writers commented at different times on shabbiness and neglect evident in Ely and could well have said something similar in the 1960s. The Ely as of 1962 was considerably smaller than today with a popuation of under 10,000 but as children we were always told that Ely, although so small, was a city because it had a cathedral. Any ambiguity about its status is explained by tensions between traditional local government arrangements and ecclesiastical leadership. The abbey was re-founded in the tenth century and special 'freedoms' accorded by charter at that time. Further charters were conferred by Edward the Confessor and William I.

Bishops in Ely have had more authority than is usual, initially powers that would have belonged to the King, and later to secular administration and explain why the church ran legal processes and courts in the Isle of Ely until the late-1830s. In papers and maps Ely across the years Ely is usually referred to as a city. I left Ely in 1973 for teacher training college in London and it was therefore a surprise to learn that Ely was only formally granted city status by Queen Elizabeth II in 1974, after I had left. Throughout my childhood and teenage years we never referred to Ely as East Cambridgeshire. We always spoke of Cambridgeshire and the Isle of Ely.

At the core of Ely is the cathedral with its ecclesiastical buildings to the south down a road called the Gallery with the Porta, the original entrance to the old monastery, at the far end. By the 1960s many of these buildings belonged to the King's School and many more historical buildings have been taken over by the school since. On the Cathedral Green the fifteenth century Bishop's Palace had become a residential children's home run by the Red Cross. An early eighteenth-century house stood opposite, walled and gated. The military cannon on its metal carriage, captured at Sebastopol in the Crimean War and gifted to Ely by Queen Victoria in 1860, marking the creation of Ely Volunteer Rifles, stood in the middle of the green. To the north of the cathedral is the Lamb hotel where I spent the summer of 1975 as a kitchen hand. At that time the Lamb had seen better days as a coaching inn from the mid-eighteenth century. The High Street and Market Street, parallel roads on either side of the Lamb, both led, as they still do, to the market square which in 1962 still had a Corn Exchange and Public Room built in in the 1840s. My mother remembered three cinemas in Ely – one in the Public Room where she said there had also been dancing. To the west of the cathedral was St Mary's Church, Cromwell's House, and the Thomas Parsons' almshouses where my mother lived for the last eight years of her life, set up and owned by the Thomas Parsons charity which dated to the fifteenth century. The square of almshouses was designed by George Basevi, the architect of the Fitzwilliam Museum in Cambridge and built in the 1860s. (In 1847, the British architect, George Gilbert Scott, was appointed to renovate Ely Cathedral, a project which continued for most of his life – his longest association. My ancestors must have been very aware of the works.) When visiting one of the almshouses as a child I was struck by the smallness of each house. They were more like bedsits with a sleeping area demarked by a curtain that was closed during the day. They were extensively modernised many years later.

Ely in the 1960s was on the cusp of new developments, not all for the better. There had been some developments in the early years of the twentieth century with the building of residential buildings along the A10 towards Littleport including some terraces but stopping far short of the RAF base which was equidistant between the cathedral, at Chettisham, a village further along the road with a distinctive wheat silo building. To the south housing stopped well short of the river and railway station and there was nothing beyond the cemetery in Prickwillow Road or beyond West Fen Road. The Corn Exchange and Public Room would be demolished in 1965, when planning was very cavalier, to make way for an unremarkable parade of shops which remains today.

1960s Ely felt isolated, unloved and down-at-heel and on-the-cusp of new developments. The annual funfair installed itself on the market square with rides and stalls in front of the Public Rooms, circling around in front of the old colonnaded Corn Exchange building. I remember sitting on its low steps with a transparent plastic bag containing a goldfish while my father pitched to win me a prize. He won. The prize was a tall doll with a disc in its back which enabled it to say, 'Hello, I am Jackie.' We walked home with our prizes, my mother warning that all trips to the fair wouldn't be like this one. There would be new developments in the 1960s: our first proper public library opened in 1966 on a corner of the Cathedral Green. Until then there was a small room in Bray's Lane that opened on specific afternoons. A new police station was built on the corner of Lynn Road and Nutholt Lane, replacing the colonnaded Victorian Shire Hall in Lynn Road. On Thursdays there was always a cattle market which as children we went to whenever there was a school holiday, settling ourselves down on the raked wooden seats watching the auctioning of cattle, sheep and pigs in the main auction space in the morning, and checking out the rabbits, hens and other smaller animals in the afternoon. At some point the market was demolished to be replaced by a Waitrose.

Beyond the centre, a mile to the north, was an RAF base with a hospital which was used by local people. To the south was an outdoor swimming pool in Angel Drove and beyond the railway station, which felt cut off from the main town. Much later efforts were made to make the Great River Ouse part of the town. In the early 1970s the Maltings building was renovated and transformed into a venue but only in the late 1990s was there any concerted effort to bring the river into public use with a millennium park, river walks and facilities.

In my memory there was no sense at all that the place had a past. The centre of the Ely of the 1960s was substantially the same as it had been in Rhoda and John Clements' time. In 1960 the city had a population of around 10,000 at the time. Even today with a population of nearer 20,000 the residential growth – which now extends to the re-routed A10 and ring road – is not obvious to the casual visitor whose focus is on the area immediately around the cathedral and towards the river Great Ouse. In fact the compact centre of Ely has become a conservation area with efforts made to capitalise on the old city and consolidate its heritage status. Today there are walks and green spaces that did not exist in the 1960s.

The Cambridgeshire Fens take up around 200 square miles within a wider Fenland which also includes Lincolnshire and some of Norfolk. The land is black and flat, mostly below sea level and due south of the Wash, which is England's largest tidal estuary. The area was covered in water until the seventeenth century with a few 'islands' which were higher and were inhabited but only accessible by boat. Monastic settlements had been built across the area in medieval times as Christian groups were attracted to the isolation. There were monastic settlements in Ely, Thorney, Croyland, Ramsey and Peterborough which together are called the 'Fen Five'. The monasteries were wealthy and kept the waterways open and the area navigable. As early as the thirteenth century they had re-routed the Great Ouse as part of land drainage. Local people survived by catching fish, waterfowl and eels. Eels in particular were a local currency at the time of the monasteries, and could be used to settle debts or pay rent. Working people harvested reeds and osiers which were used for making baskets, traps and pots. They adapted to local conditions, farmed the common lands, and developed ways to hunt waterfowl, eels and fish, to extract peat and graze cattle and sheep. They built up resistance to endemic diseases including a type of malaria called Fen Ague. When the monasteries were dissolved in the mid-sixteenth century no one picked up the responsibility for drainage again until the seventeenth century when King James I and King Charles I saw a financial benefit in transforming what they saw as a vast wasteland into rich agricultural land: I will discuss this later.

CHAPTER 1

The History – the Isle of Ely: 'A far greater country'

'You have only to open your eyes to be convinced that England must have been a far greater and more wealthy country in those days than it is in these days.'
William Cobbett, *Rural Rides* (1830)

William Cobbett (1763-1835) visited Ely and wrote about his visit to the Cambridgeshire Fens in his *Rural Rides* (1830), his most famous publication. He had reason to be curious about Ely as *'the place where the flogging of the English local militia under a guard of German bayonets cost me so dear'*. In 1810 Cobbett had been found guilty of treasonous libel following comments he made in in his *Political Register* in July 1809 about a violent incident in Ely. He had publicly condemned the flogging of members of the local militia, mustered for training in Ely, who had complained openly about having the cost of their knapsacks deducted from their pay. The 'mutiny' was broken up by four squadrons of German Legion calvary (these were expatriate German soldiers formed between 1803 and 1816, to fight the French Napoleonic wars). Five men had been identified as ring-leaders and had each been sentenced to 500 lashes delivered by the German Legion then quartered in Bury St Edmunds. For opposing this in print Cobbett was given a two-year sentence to be served in Newgate Prison and a £1000 fine. On his visit to Ely some twenty years later he was keen to see where the floggings had taken place *'and to find some opportunity or other of relating the story as publicly as I could at Ely, and of describing the tail of the story'* (Vol 2, 229). Cobbett found a local man who took him to the place where the floggings had happened, *'a little common along which the men had been marched, and into a piece of pasture-land, where he put his foot upon the identical spot where the flogging had been executed.'* Cobbett also located one of the two Ely men who were among the five who were flogged, and found him, *'very nice-looking, and appears to be a hard-working man, and to bear an excellent character.'* Cobbett described Ely as 'a miserable little town: very prettily situated, but poor and mean' with the cathedral in *'disgraceful irrepair and disfigurement'*. He reflected that a thousand years earlier it had been very different as the existence of Ely Cathedral testified – he particularly regretted the dissolution of the monasteries. On the occasion of his visit, as he was very keen to impart '*the tail of the story*' of the floggings to the local men, he gathered some in one of Ely's inns. He explained to them that English money from taxes was, as a consequence of the flogging episode, being sent to the Germans, thus impoverishing local people.

ELY CATHEDRAL FROM BARTON SQUARE TODAY

Ely's early history

Ely is now considered a desirable place to live but it had peaked in importance a long time ago and many centuries before William Cobbett's visit. Its city status dates from 1109, the abbey having attained cathedral status in 1108 and its abbot a bishoprick. Before then, in 673, a monastery was founded by Etheldreda, a seventh century princess, the daughter of King Anna of East Anglia. There had already been a religious settlement at Cratendune, a 'lost village' south of Ely, founded, apparently, in 607, but Etheldreda opted for a site a mile north, probably in an area of Ely around today's St John's Road, at a higher point than Cratendune, for her mixed community of monks and nuns. In Ely's West End a small group of medieval buildings, formerly the 'hospitals' (probably hostelries) of St John Baptist and St Mary Magdalene, remain on the site.

Growing up in Ely I remember well the thirteenth centenary celebrations in 1973 when there was a huge public party in Ely Park and when the BBC filmed *It's a Knockout*, a television gameshow starting in 1966, which featured different British towns competing in a sort of adult school sports day format. The Ely team went through to the European Final, *Jeux sans frontières* in Paris that year. There was a season of arts and sporting events. Our girls' and boys' grammar schools in Ely and nearby Soham had been converted to comprehensives by then and the recently formed City of Ely Sixth Form College put on a production of Gilbert and Sullivan's *The Mikado*, with Koko including the '*Ely Festivalist*' on his song containing a '*little list of society offenders who never would be missed*'. That Autumn I left Ely for teacher training college but without a strong sense that I understood much of Ely's history. As Cobbett had said, the presence of the cathedral was evidence to those of us living there in the 1960s and 1970s of Ely's earlier splendour, an importance that we could only imagine.

With one exception, which I will discuss in Chapters 3 and 4, all my ancestors were born and lived in the County of Cambridgeshire. The 'Isle of Ely' where most of them originated is a raised area of land which is part of Cambridgeshire but has been independent in the past. The Isle itself is the biggest of a number of raised areas within an area of marshland with Ely to the East, Aldreth on the far south-west. Little Downham to the north and including the villages of Mepal, Sutton, Haddenham and Witchford. Other smaller 'isles' included Littleport and Stuntney. Until the seventeenth century most of the engagement with the Isle of Ely would have been by river making the riverside area of the Great Ouse an important trading part of the city, and the focus for trade being between the river and the cathedral.

The History – the Isle of Ely: 'A far greater country'

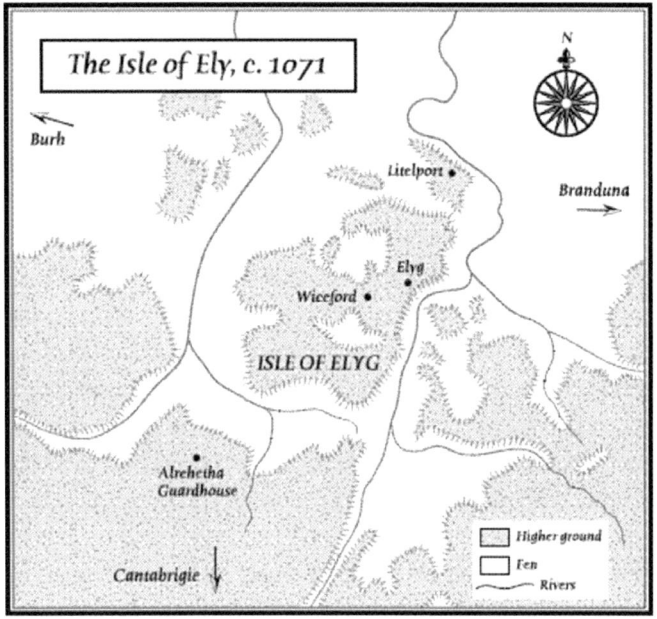

MAP OF THE ISLE OF ELY, C. 1071

Until the seventeenth century the Isle was surrounded by water and marshy land that was either permanently or seasonally flooded. The places where my family members lived, like Ely, Littleport, Soham, Stuntney and Whittlesey, all feature in the Domesday Book of 1087 when the Abbey of Ely, founded in 673 but re-founded as a Benedictine monastery by St Ethelwold and St Dunstan in 970 (and made a bishopric in 1109) was one of the richest landowners in the country. Some say it was only surpassed in wealth by Glastonbury. Others say that the abbeys of York and Bury St Edmunds were wealthier. Norwich was a bigger place with 1358 households, the second biggest city in the country after London, but Ely with 92 households was still in the top 20% of English places and its abbey owned land throughout

Cambridgeshire, Suffolk, Norfolk and Huntingdonshire. Ely's name is said to comes from the local eels. It recorded 3750 eels in Domesday. Eels were an important indicator of wealth in the Domesday Book, not only in the Fens, and used in lieu of cash payments or as evidence of wealth. Littleport and Stuntney, both smaller villages on their own 'islands' outside Ely, contributed 24,000 eels apiece every year to the Abbot of Ely. It seems that the monks and nuns in the local monasteries were kept well supplied with local produce including eels and game by the local people probably as tithes or rent payments. The Barnack stone from Northamptonshire with which Ely Cathedral was built, and which was transported to Ely by river, was said to have been purchased with 8,000 eels per year. There is now an annual Eel Festival in Ely, a recent 'tradition'.

King Cnut's visits to the fens

The *Liber Eliensis is* a twelfth century account of the history of the Fens from 673 to the twelfth century. It was written in Latin by two Ely monks from the Abbey at Ely. One tale it tells is of King Cnut, the Danish king (born 994) who ruled England, Denmark, and Norway from 1016 to 1035, and whose basis was Wessex (he was to be buried in Winchester Cathedral) who was a frequent visitor to the Isle of Ely with his queen, Emma. The visits were ostensibly to celebrate the Purification of St Mary (February 2) but it seems likely that they may have been a result of some resistance to his reign and the need to check up on potential uprisings. *Liber Eliensis* makes much of the fact that the Isle of Ely was surrounded by water and that on several occasions 'the king was unable to come to this festival because of the excessive frost and ice in the locality, the marshes and meres being frozen all around.' (*Liber Eliensis,* Book II, 85) On one occasion he decided to 'travel all the way to Ely over the mere from Soham in a wagon upon the ice'.

King Cnut is credited with a poem about Ely and the beginning of it is quoted in *Liber Eliensis (II,85),*

> The monks in Ely sweetly sang
> When nigh rowed Cnut the King.
> Knights, row closer to the land
> And let's hear these monks sing!

On another occasion Cnut travelled to Ely only to find that the monks had fallen into bad ways and, because they were inebriated, failed to recognise him or offer hospitality. He went along the River Ouse to Littleport where he found a welcome and a supper of eels. He vowed to put things right at the Abbey returning it to its former religious practices – the monks' misdemeanours seem to have included a fair amount of womanising with the locals.

Cnut was succeeded by his son Harthacnut (reigned 1035-42) and then by Edward the Confessor (reigned 1042-1066). Edward was educated at the Kings' School in Ely at a time when Ely had a thriving abbey community which was amongst the richest in the country. Nigel, Bishop of Ely (1122-69), was Treasurer of England for King Henry 1 before his appointment to Ely and very influential at court throughout his life, and as Bishop played a controversial role in national politics by supporting King Stephen's rival to the throne, Matilda, before becoming reconciled with Stephen and present at his coronation in 1141. Nigel was an early proponent of fen drainage, and built a castle in Ely, 'a strong fort of lime and stone', probably near the river where Castlehythe is today. There were castles at Aldreth and on Ely's Cherry Hill, built by the Normans, but there is little trace of any of them today.

The authors of the *Liber Eliensis* were not enthusiastic about Nigel, who they claimed 'needed to raise money in order to repair his own political fortunes' and that he sold many of Ely's monastic treasures. Subsequent bishops of Ely held high offices in the State and particularly as Lord Chancellors and Lord Treasurers.

The abbeys and monasteries

There was a revival of monastic building in the 970s across the wider Fens following the earlier destruction of the original ecclesiastical buildings by raiders from across the North Sea, the Danes. They had undoubtedly heard about the wealth of the East Anglian abbeys. The Fenland Benedictine abbeys of Ely, Ramsey, Crowland, Thorney and Peterborough all date from this time. These monasteries owned land and farms, and after the Romans, who built canals across the region for navigational, rather than drainage purposes, were the first to drain parts of the Fens to make the area more habitable.

The *Liber Eliensis* tells us that Etheldreda owned the Isle of Ely and managed it. In the tenth century the 'Liberty of Ely' was established by King Edgar, confirmed in 1052 by King Edward the Confessor, and then, after Hereward's departure, by William I. Hereward the Wake, an eleventh century nobleman, held out against the Normans in the Isle of Ely in 1071, which was possible because the Isle's higher ground was only accessible via the three causeways through Earith, Stuntney, and Aldreth, the latter two managed by the monks at the monastery. There are different versions of Hereward's story: in one account he allowed the Normans to approach the Isle by one of the causeways, probably Aldreth, which was covered with sedge. When the Norman soldiers were halfway across the causeway he set fire to the sedge, driving them back. Another version has the Normans sinking on the causeway because of the weight of their horses and armour. Most agree that monks from the abbey, believing that the Abbey's interests rested with the King, informed the Norman soldiers of a safe way into the Isle, forcing Hereward to flee.

When my then school, Ely High School for Girls, was established in Ely in 1905, it named its four house groups Etheldreda, Hereward, Cnut and Alan. Alan of Walsingham oversaw the building of the octagon tower of Ely Cathedral after the collapse of the original central tower in 1322.

OUTSIDE ELY

Administration of the area was always separate from the usual local government systems, an arrangement that lasted until the reign of Edward IV. In my childhood in the 1960s we still talked about 'Cambridgeshire and the Isle of Ely' until, for administrative reasons, the Isle was incorporated within the county of Cambridgeshire in 1965. In my memory the Isle of Ely was separate from everywhere possibly because of its island nature and somewhat isolated history. It was very clear when you left the city itself because, whichever way you looked, you could see only expansive black fields with roads edged by dykes and drains. The rivers are still mostly embanked, and railways and villages are often built on 'rodhams' (a word first cited in *OED* in 185), i.e. on old dried out clay-filled river beds above the level of the surrounding land, so that fenland landscapes are marked out by uninterrupted lines with long straight roads without hedges or walls. Towns and villages have expanded but the Fen itself is farming land disrupted only by occasional farmhouses surrounded by small clumps of trees that are absent elsewhere. Today's landscape reflects the area's more recent 'reclaimed' history as the 'bread basket' for the nation.

The early drainage projects

Although as a child I assumed that the countryside around Ely was a natural phenomenon the Fens as we know them today are the result of centuries of drainage interventions. Almost all the rivers in the area have been re-routed, dredged and drained many times over centuries, sometimes successfully but as often pushed back by new floods or storms. The earliest drainage projects were very local ones to improve navigation in the immediate area. It was not in landowners' interests to go beyond their personal holdings and often farmers' improvements on their own property caused problems for farmers elsewhere. Before the dissolution of the monasteries the Abbeys took responsibility for the drainage but these fell into disrepair. Later speculators saw the potential for increased value and personal profit in larger schemes aiming to drain the entire region, replacing marshes with agricultural land. The drainage schemes needed to address both the threat of the North Sea at the Wash to the north as well as freshwater floods from the storms and overflowing rivers flowing into the area from the Midlands. Until then the unusual juxtaposition of salt and fresh water on a watery landscape created a unique eco-system with meres which were lowland lakes, flooded grasslands and occasional dry islands which were habitable. Grazing animals could be relocated to dry lands in the winter – dominated in medieval times by sheep farming. With the dissolution of the monasteries by Henry VIII in the 1530s these lands were distributed to new owners who already had an eye to making them profitable. In

1601 in the reign of Elizabeth I there was an act 'for the recovering of many thousand acres of marshes, and other grounds…within the Isle of Ely, and in the counties of Huntingdon, Northampton, Lincoln, Norfolk, Suffolk, Sussex, Essex, Kent and the County Palatine of Durham.' (Darby, 444). This was the beginning of a period when it was legally possible to give up land to speculators which would finance drainage projects in return for ownership of the resulting drained fields. The early schemes were met with vehement objections from the local people.

The Fens as we have them today are the result of centuries of drainage interventions. The story we were told as schoolchildren of a single drainage project overseen by the Dutch engineer Cornelius Vermuyden (1595-1677) was an over-simplification. Almost all the rivers in the area have been re-routed, dredged and drained many times over centuries, sometimes successfully but as often pushed back by new floods or storms. The earliest drainage projects were very local ones to improve navigation in the immediate area. It was not in landowners' interests to go beyond their personal holdings and often farmers' improvements on their own property caused problems for farmers elsewhere. Later speculators saw the potential for increased value and personal profit in larger schemes aiming to drain the entire region, replacing marshes with agricultural land. The drainage schemes needed to address both the threat of the North Sea at the Wash to the north as well as freshwater floods from the storms and overflowing rivers flowing into the area from the Midlands. Until then the unusual juxtaposition of salt and fresh water on a watery landscape created a unique eco-system with meres, which were lowland lakes, flooded grasslands and occasional dry islands which were habitable. Grazing animals could be relocated to dry lands in the winter – dominated in medieval times by sheep farming. With the dissolution of the monasteries by Henry VIII in the 1530s these lands were distributed to new owners who already had an eye to making them profitable. In 1601 in the reign of Elizabeth I there was an act 'for the recovering of many thousand acres of marshes, and other grounds...within the Isle of Ely, and in the counties of Huntingdon, Northampton, Lincoln, Norfolk, Suffolk, Sussex, Essex, Kent and the County Palatine of Durham.' (Darby, 444). This was the beginning of a period when it was legally possible to give up land to speculators which would finance drainage projects in return for land. The early schemes were met with vehement objections from the local people.

Drainage under the Stuart Kings

It was during the reigns of the Stuart Kings that the Fenland drainage projects took off. King James I (reigned 1603-1625) started to see marshlands as a means of raising funds including in Hatfield Chase in Yorkshire where rivers were re-routed and drains laid on a financial model that rewarded the King and local landowners, but also 'adventurers' who invested as speculators. These Jacobean schemes which promised quick riches were parodied by Ben Jonson in his play, *The Devil is an Ass* (1616) where Fitzdottrell, a squire of Norfolk, is taunted by Merecraft,

WICKED FEN WHERE THE PRE-DRAINAGE
LANDSCAPE HAS BEEN PRESERVED

a Projector, with the possibility making money and of becoming 'Duke of the Drowned-Lands' or 'Duke of Drowned-Land'. 'Ha', says Fitzdorrell, 'That last had a good sound! I like it well. The Duke of Drowned-Land?......It goes like Greenland, sir, if you mark it.' (Ben Jonson, *The Devil is an Ass*, Act 2, Scene 4, 22-23). He likes the title and tells his wife,

> This man defies the Devil, and all his works!
> He does't by engine and devices, he!
> He has his winged ploughs that go with sails,
> Will plough you forty acres at once! All Crowland
> Is ours, wife; and the fens, from us in Norfolk
> To the utmost bound of Lincolnshire! We have viewed it,
> And measured it within all, by the scale!
> The richest tract of land, love, i' the kingdom!
> There will be made seventeen, or eighteen millions;
> Or more, as 't may be handled!'
> Ben Jonson, *The Devil is an Ass*, Act 2, Scene 3, 46-55

A group of 'adventurers', proto-venture capitalists, led by Francis Russell, 4th Earl of Bedford (1587-1641) who owned land near Thorney and Whittlesey, initiated the bigger Fenland projects. In the 1630s he and his fellow investors transacted to drain and maintain drained lands in exchange for ninety-five thousand acres which included an allocation to the King, by now Charles I (reigned 1625-1649), and as a result the Bedford Level Corporation received its charter in 1634. The Dutchman Cornelius Vermuyden was already known for his successes in the Hatfield Levels in Yorkshire and in Dagenham on the north side of the River Thames, and possibly in Canvey Island in Essex, and had been knighted in 1629 becoming a British citizen soon after. He was contracted to the Fen project but his relationship with the adventurers seems to have been turbulent. The Fenland project proved challenging. Costs were hard to control and there were disputes about what had been agreed, leading Charles I to revoke the contract taking back responsibility to the Crown in 1638. Some work, including Vermuyden's plan to create a 21-mile long channel, now known as the Old Bedford River and other 'cuts' in different rivers, was completed and the adventurers received their 40,000 acres.

Impact of the drainage projects on local people

Local people in the Fens were, inevitably, suspicious of proposals to radically change their landscape, livelihoods and way of life. They knew how to navigate the wetlands, including being adept at travelling around on stilts, and in fishing punts, which were flat-bottomed boats ideal for navigating shallow water. Today punts are most commonly used by tourists punting along the Backs on the River Cam in Cambridge but fishing punts would have been armed with a punt gun, i.e. a large shotgun mounted on the end of the punt that could be fired at numbers of wildfowl at one time, the boatman lying flat along the length of the punt, often killing forty or fifty birds at a time. Fen farmers were able to pasture their cattle in the summer and move the animals on to dry ground in the winter. In addition to fishing and fowling local men collected sedge which could be used for thatching and basket-making. The prospect of this way of life changing was a threat to livelihoods. There was much formal lobbying and petitioning by the local people which went to the very top of Government. There were anti-drainage demonstrations, legal appeals and riots throughout the Fenland towns including Littleport, Ely, Coveney and Wicken. There was sabotaging of the drainage works themselves. Progress with the drainage projects was disrupted by the civil war (1642-1651), by cashflow problems and by shortages of labour – solved by bringing in Scottish prisoners after the Battle of Dunbar (1650) and Dutch prisoners later because local people would not get involved. Around 11,000 men are believed to have been involved in the digging out of the Old and New Bedford rivers. In 1652 Cornelius Vermuyden declared that 'the area now known as the Bedford Level has been well and truly drained', and on 26 March 1653, optimistically – because there would be many more problems ahead – a general thanksgiving for the completion of the works was held in Ely Cathedral.

Vermuyden's legacy

Cornelius Vermuyden disappeared from the records at this point other than being visible through documents about land interests that he had collected over a career of drainage projects and used speculatively to raise money when he could, and by records of his children's well-to-do marriages, but we know he died in Westminster in 1677. The New and Old Bedford canals had been cut creating an expanse of some 19 miles between the two, which, because of the clever construction of higher outer banks of the two channels, acted as an overflow and reservoir when floods threatened. Peter Scott, the son of the Antarctic explorer, set up a wildlife centre in Welney by the new rivers in the 1940s, which my father took me to as a child. The Great Ouse was contained within two sluices at Earith in the south and Denver in the north and became the drain for its tributaries, the Cam, the Lark, the Little Ouse and the Wissey. From the late 1650s the area became rich agricultural land for flax, hemp, oats, wheat, cole-seed and woad. A network of 'cuts', drains, river re-routings and sluices had been created to transform the large expanse of Fenland into profitable farming land, changing its character and eco-system completely and forever.

Daniel Defoe (1660-1731), who made a *'Tour through the Eastern Counties of England'*, in 1722 nearly a century earlier than Cobbett, pointed out that *'all the waters of the middle part of England which does not run into the Thames or the Trent, comes down into these fens'*, and indeed it is true that the Fenland rivers of which the Great Ouse is the biggest, were regularly inundated by all the rivers of middle England, and because the rivers flow through the flat lands with only small gradients, they could not disperse these flows into the Wash to the north quickly enough to avoid flooding.

Finishing the job

This was not the end of the story. There would continue to be periodic flooding, the which followed from maintenance being carried out badly or the effect of bad winters, and because the drained lands in the Cambridgeshire area revealed rich peat that shrank over time, they required other inventions to pump the waters up from the land, initially windmills, which Daniel Defoe described as 'wonderful engines for throwing up water'. These were

THE CAMBRIDGESHIRE FENS TODAY

followed by steam pumps, then diesel; and today electrically driven pumps work in the background day and night to keep the Fenlands functioning. The flat fields today are separated by water channels which flow into dykes and drains and into the outflows which are then pumped up into the rivers which are above the roads and fields.

The 1947 Floods

The Great Floods of 1947 were still a folk memory in my childhood. My mother who was twenty-two at the time remembered them well and they were often mentioned in our family. Controversies between landowners, drainage boards and local councils, over who was responsible for repairs and drainage of the Fens had continued into the twentieth century and important improvements were delayed by the second world war and then put off again by disagreements about what needed doing and how much could be spent. In 1947 the winter was severe and the snow did not melt until March. Heavy rains meant that it was inevitable that the river banks would be breached, and that a wide area of Fenland would be inundated. In the South Level – Cambridgeshire – 37,000 acres were under water following the worst floods in living memory. When the crisis was over, lessons were learnt, and the rebuilding was more ambitious than had previously been planned. As a child I remember regular flooding of houses opposite our house, on the A10 road that ran between Ely and Littleport The houses were lower than the road and neighbours had to bale out the water. Memories of the 1947 floods meant that people living in the Fens were always conscious of the possibility of more flooding and the complicated water engineering systems that kept the area stable.

CHAPTER 2

Education

With the exception of one family member, my mother's great-grandfather, Allen Owen, who came to Whittlesey from Cheadle, near Manchester, to work for Eastern Counties Railway (ECR) in the mid-nineteenth century, everyone in my both my parents' families was born in the Fens.

Most of them came from an area of about 17,000 acres edged by Littleport, Prickwillow and Ely, known as Burnt Fen which is a small area mostly in Cambridgeshire but spilling out to Norfolk in the north, and West Suffolk to the east. The area is hemmed in by three rivers, the Great Ouse, the Little Ouse and the Lark, and mostly given over to agricultural use with very few houses and fewer traces of the area's history. The Littleport-Mildenhall road crosses through the area north-west to south-east and the Ely-Norwich railway, built in 1845, crosses east to west with Shippea Hill station, until 1904 called Burnt Fen Station, and now a famously unbusy station with only a handful of passengers recorded each year, mostly generated when the station gets occasional publicity and railway station enthusiasts are prompted to visit it as Britain's least used station. The station stands isolated, slightly higher than the surrounding fields which are below sea level with one train each weekday going to Norwich in the morning.

Since 1759 when the agricultural potential of the area was first recognised, Burnt Fen has been managed by the Commissioners of the Burnt Fen District and is completely dependent on pumped drainage with some 40 miles of ditches serviced by two pumping stations located on the River Lark and Great Ouse which 'lift' water up into the rivers. During Vermuyden's time rivers in the area were re-routed but with drainage came peat shrinkage. Windmills were brought in to power the original pumps but were superseded by steam and then diesel.

Three of my parents' families came from this area and without exception the men were agricultural workers whose working life began at the age of thirteen or fourteen. There is little trace of them before the eighteenth century but we can assume that, as the land became workable and farmers started to move in, the labourers followed. A pumping mill was installed at Brandon Creek in 1832, and another near the River Lark near Prickwillow in 1842, to be replaced by steam in the late 1880s. My ancestors lived through these improvements, moving to the area from Littleport in the north and Mildenhall to the east in the 1820s and settled there for the duration of the nineteenth century and into the twentieth. Their lives as agricultural workers were more or less unchanged from 1820 until after the First World War, after which they gravitated into the City of Ely and its environs.

Those of us who were born in the 1940s and 1950s, the Baby Boomers, were only the second generation of people in the UK who were able to do better than their parents in terms of long-term earnings and opportunities. This was true of the Fens as elsewhere. Selina Todd, in *Snakes & Ladders: The Great British Social Mobility Myth* (Penguin, 2021) destroys the myth that each generation naturally exceeds the achievements of the previous one. Until my generation few of my Fenland ancestors improved on their parents' social class or earnings; many went in the opposite direction. Without exception the men in my family were agricultural labourers and from the 1880s most of the women went into service as maids or cooks from their teens and up until the time of their marriages. Few members of my family left the Fens but those who did, went far away with no expectation of returning. A few emigrated in the 1850s, voluntarily to North America, or forcibly to New South Wales and fared better than they would have done at home. Later in the nineteenth century some were recruited to the major Victorian infrastructure projects: to the iron ore mines on Tyneside or building Joseph Bazalgette's sewage systems in East Ham in east London. They too did not return and there is little evidence that they stayed in contact with their families back in Cambridgeshire. There was almost no movement out of the Fens by my family in the twentieth century other than as soldiers, who either died in conflicts or returned to the Fens to circumstances no better off, and sometimes worse than they left. My great-uncle, Ephraim Clements, was one such; he left Prickwillow to join the 4th Suffolk Regiment in Bury St Edmunds when he was nineteen in 1893, serving in India, Rangoon and on the North-West Frontier before being sent to South Africa as part of the Second Boer War. His army career was peppered with disciplinary issues, and on his return to Prickwillow after a decade in the army he was regularly in the local press for drunkenness and abusive behaviour until his early death in 1911 at the age of thirty-seven. There is little evidence of him holding down a job. His sister, my great-aunt Rhoda Clements was persuaded by another brother who had left the Fens, following an uncle who had made a living in the North-East in the great Iron-ore rush, to become a maid to a retired bachelor, a Master Mariner, and his sister, in the late 1880s. She married her employer in 1897 and her fortunes seemed to have improved but she died in Morpeth County Asylum at the age of forty-two in 1908.

My generation was the first to benefit from free secondary school education following the 1944 Education Act. Unlike those who had gone before who were at elementary schools throughout their school years and left school at thirteen or fourteen, my generation were all able to complete secondary education. The generations after mine may have benefited from the opportunity to go to university but by then were faced with student loans to repay and precarious job opportunities. In the Fens as elsewhere, Margaret Thatcher's 1982 Housing Act enabled some families the 'Right to Buy' their council houses at a discount and improve the social position of one generation but it also meant that there was no subsidised housing for those that followed by which time social housing carried a stigma that had not been there in the past. According to Selina Todd (2014, p.175) 'almost one-third of British Households [rented their home from a council] by the 1970s'. The Government's own data for 2020 gave the latest figure as 17% with the Local Government Association estimating that 2.1 million families were on waiting lists. By the 1980s public sector 'jobs for life', which had benefited working class Baby Boomers were rare, following public sector cuts which would be exacerbated in the 2010s with austerity measures leading to a culture of freelance or sessional working for the better off and 'zero hours contracts' for the poorest. My parents' generation lived in rented housing all their lives: my generation following them were the first to own their own houses.

The post-war growth of the welfare state, National Health Service (1948) and access to free secondary schools education required an army of new employees, many of whom came from young people who were the first in their families to stay on at school until eighteen or move into Further or Higher Education, or into Teacher Training which was an option until teaching became an all-graduate profession in the late 1970s. As sixth-former, the girls in my school were encouraged into teaching and about a third of my year group went on to Teacher Training College where we gained Certificates in Education, not degrees. Many girls left school at eighteen and went into employment as trainee accountants or as office workers. A very few went to university. (Thus, of my friends, Rosemary Russell went into teacher-training, Judy Lemn (married name Cullum), and Elaine Lawrence went into accounting, and Frances Hatch did modern languages, and. became a painter. Even in a grammar school some girls left at sixteen for unskilled work or to marry and start their families. Things were slightly better for boys. Teaching had a reputation. In 1946 an Emergency Teacher Train Scheme had been introduced to address the need for teachers to be in place for the 1947 raising of the school leaving age to fifteen which required 30,000 extra teachers. Twenty-three thousand men and twelve thousand women qualified under the Scheme and by 1955 42% of primary school teachers were from the homes of manual workers. Teaching was becoming a profession of people that had been upwardly mobile and for many its attraction was to support young people from similar backgrounds.

In common with forty per cent of English workers in 1850 my ancestors worked on the land. By 1881 only 13% were agricultural workers but this smaller group also included most of the men and boys, and some of the girls and women, in my Fenland family. By the 1880s the girls were expected to take up servant positions from the age of thirteen, either working for local families or further afield. In doing so they were in the company of 43% of women in service at the time mostly working for the expanding middle classes who could afford one or two girls who did everything for the household from clearing the grates in the morning, to cooking and laundry and childcare. Their only escape from service was to marry and most settled as wives of farm labourers by the time they were in their mid-twenties.

My father, the youngest of my grandparents' six children, started out as a farm worker when he left elementary school at the age of fourteen but soon followed his brother into the Suffolk Regiment as a regular soldier, signing up as soon as he could at the age of eighteen in 1937. His brother, thirteen years older, had enrolled with the same regiment in 1923, also at the age of eighteen, and judging from my collection of his tiny photographs brought back from postings abroad, my father would have grown up hearing stories about Malta, Gilbraltar, Shanghai, Cairo and Hong Kong, and perhaps thought that this life would be better than a lifetime as an agricultural labourer in Cambridgeshire. The Suffolk Regiment was long-established (starting in 1685), and attracted recruits from across East Anglia including Cambridgeshire. Its Gilbraltar Barracks, still there today with a small regimental museum, in Bury St Edmunds, was built as a recruiting and training centre in 1878.

My father almost certainly had not considered that the country would go to war in September 1939 by which time he was posted with the 2nd Battalion of the Suffolk Regiment at Mhow in Madhya Pradesh in India. Mhow was a well-established army base dating back to the mid-nineteenth century and by the 1940s was a large garrison town. During the second world war the place was overrun with troops either on 'rest or recovery' or training for the expected war in Burma (Myanmar). In the November my father's regiment was moved up to Razmak, on the North West Frontier, now part of Pakistan, where they were on internal security duties. In October 1943 the Battalion joined the 123rd Indian Infantry Bridgade taking part in the Burma campaign including the Arakan and Imphal. When the war ended the regiment stayed on at Lahore in present-day Pakistan. My father was decommissioned in 1947 after ten years of army service and he returned to the Fens with five military medals and a certificate saying he had qualified as a driver, but with no formal qualifications or increased opportunities.

There had been a charity school for boys – apprentices mainly – established through the legacy of Catherine Needham in the mid-eighteenth century with a building which still stands on Back Hill and is now an arts block for the King's School. In my day it was an adult education institution. Over the years it became a senior school for boys before they were relocated to the National School in Silver Street which opened in 1859 as St Mary's. My father and his sisters attended St Mary's sporadically in the early years of the twentieth century, and in 1962 I started at the same school. My parents went to school until they were thirteen – the legal leaving age was fourteen at the time but none of my parents' generation seem to have stayed at school until fourteen – at which point my mother went into service and my father started working on the land.

A month before my grandfather died I started school. I was five at the end of April and started school that summer term. Opposite our house was a small cul-de-sac called St Audrey's Way with new bungalows. Beyond was a small alleyway which led to vast school fields – twenty-two acres. The girls' high school was at the far edge of the site towards Little Downham where my father's family had lived for many years, on the actual site of the school. St Audrey's infant school, the first of the school developments that had opened in 1953, was at the opposite end, near the town. There must have been ambitious plans for education in the Isle of Ely in the 1950s because that huge site had been designated as an educational campus and it was good ten-minute walk between the main entrances of the two schools.

Between the two schools the vast fields were well-maintained with hockey and netball pitches, and tennis courts. Although built in the 1950s both schools were model 1960s educational buildings in every way: floor to ceiling glass on one side making for capacious classrooms which were light and airy. There was parquet flooring throughout and halls for assembly, lunch, music, drama and PE. The girls' high school also had science laboratories, a gym with changing rooms, and a library. In 1969, a secondary modern school was added to the educational campus but there were no more developments and much of the land was subsequently sold off for residential housing. Whatever the vision had been it was not realised and today the three schools feel hemmed in by residential roads while the expansion of Ely itself has necessitated new school buildings in other parts of the town.

This was not a time when nurseries or play-groups were usual so for most of us joining St Audrey's school in 1960 it was the first time we had been parted from our mothers and for some children this was quite traumatic: some howled as they were led into their classrooms. My memories, such that they are, before starting school, are mostly of riding on a small seat on my mother's bicycle, and her advice that it was impossible to get lost in Ely or the Fens because even a child could see Ely Cathedral from wherever they strayed and return home easily. It is hard to imagine in what circumstance a child under five would have found themselves in need of this advice. For the most part my childhood until then had involved helping my mother with her housework. Our kitchen was very simple with a table, a gas cooker, a sink with a small immersion heater above, and the type of kitchen cabinet that was common at the time and which functioned as a cupboard and larder with a drop- down door that doubled as a worktop. In place of a fridge my mother had what was called a 'meat safe' which was a small wooden cupboard with mesh sides to keep out flies where meat and milk were stored. In the summer she kept milk in a bucket of water. My parents first bought a second-hand fridge in 1972, and a washing machine a couple of years before

THE AUTHOR AT ST. AUDREY'S SCHOOL, 1960

but which my mother hardly used. We never had central heating so my early memories are of my mother cleaning out the vestiges of the coal fire every morning in the winter while a portable calor gas stove provided heating. In the early 1960s my father installed a gas heater into the fireplace in the main room.

A friend of our family had started school in the January of 1960 and my mother and I walked back and forth to the school with them throughout the Spring term and I couldn't wait to be allowed to stay rather than returning alone with my mother and her friend. St Audrey's was way ahead of its time, Plowden before the wonderful 1967 Plowden Report which was our bible at teacher training college in the 1970s, with an ethos of child-centred education that must have been rare then and certainly very different to anything my parents had experienced. Not only did we learn to read and write, but there was art, music, PE and science. Maths was taught hands-on with cuisinaire rods which were boxes of brightly colour-coded rods used to work out sums practically: in the 1970s I did teaching practice in a junior school where all maths including fractions and decimals was taught with cuisinaire rods but students were not allowed to teach maths as the headteacher had developed his own particular method. Dance was taught through a BBC radio programme called 'Music and Movement' which was broadcast on Schools Radio. Because this was before recording was possible the children would need to be sitting in the school hall in vest and knickers ready for the live broadcast which entreated us to, stand, stretch, skip or jump to music, building towards some sort of imaginative response to a scene such as a storm, or windy day. Country dancing was treated equally seriously and every May there was a May Day celebration: each of the seven classes had its own maypole and its own featured dance prepared with great care. A May Queen was chosen from among the girls. Music was relayed to the field from a gramophone in one of the adjacent classrooms. Taller children from each class were required to stand with their backs to the maypole to ensure stability. The dancers would stand in a circle around the role, each with our own ribbon which would plait as the dance progressed, and then unplait.

In 1962, my final year at St Audrey's, I was a bridesmaid to my cousin Jean who married in the March of that year (she was to die there, in 2023). After the war my father worked as a labourer for Tuckers of Ely, a family-run building firm established by a prominent Methodist family in the town. The then boss lived opposite us in a new bungalow and he and his children owned almost all the houses in our terrace which was built in the 1920s, probably by his firm. My father's brother-in-law, Vic and his brother Fred, were already skilled carpenters and joiners and had worked there throughout the war. Few local men served in the war as they were key workers in an agricultural area but my father, already disillusioned by six years of farm work and inspired by his older brother who had joined the army in the 1920s, signed up as a regular soldier as soon as he could in 1937 when he was nineteen. When he was demobbed ten years later and without a job to go to my aunt persuaded her husband to put in a word for her younger brother with Fred Tucker, the boss. Tuckers had a staff of labourers and craftsmen, organised from a central office in Lynn Road, Ely. They took on all sorts of local building work, domestic and commercial. When my parents married in 1948 my father was able to secure one of Tuckers' houses to rent (120, Lynn Road).

My cousin's wedding, in the March of 1962 marked the end of almost a year of our weekend visits to a plot of land near Mildenhall. My father, and Vic and Fred had taken on the project of building the couple a bungalow on what was then a quiet country lane in a place called Beck Row, somewhere where my mother's father's family had hailed from. Now it is a high density area of new houses, many of which are owned by ex-US military families who have served at USAF Mildenhall or Lakenheath. I was one of two bridesmaids and the mother of the other made us long red velvet dresses. My long dress opened the way for me to become a maid of honour to the May Queen at our final May Day at the infants' school in 1962.

My mother and her brothers attended different schools including in Prickwillow where my father's family had lived until the beginning of the twentieth century. Insofar as could determine where our family came from, it was Prickwillow although no one lived in the village itself but in houses linked to farms in the fen. Some say the village of Prickwillow was named after the 'prickets' of willow which could be collected there and used for pinning down thatch. My mother's family had moved about the Fens: they had also lived in Whistle Drove, near Stuntney, which was a drove off one of the original causeways that had provided access from across the flooded Fens to Ely itself before the drainage projects in the seventeenth century. Stuntney was registered in the

PRICKWILLOW SCHOOL TODAY, NOW IN PRIVATE HANDS

Domesday Book as an eel fishing port, and was one of the oldest island settlements in the Fens, well-known for its shire horses. The family also lived at Queen Adelaide, a village between Ely and Prickwillow. All these places were in Burnt Fen, extending in the north to Littleport and the rivers Little and Great Ouse near the Norfolk border, and south almost to Soham near the Suffolk border. It had come into being as a result of the drainage and was overseen by the Burnt Fen Internal Drainage Board which exists to this day because without constant pumping the area would revert to its pre-drainage state.

All in all, I was lucky to attend that very enlightened infant school, St Audrey's, which, much like Sure Start in the early 2000s, about the best thing in the Blair government of 1997 onwards, gave me and my generation a headstart with reading, writing and arithmetic and conveyed a sense of opportunity and expectation. Not so my junior school which had not been touched by progressive education, and my experience there cannot have been very different from that of my father's generation except that it was by then a junior school, not an elementary school, and we left at eleven. Thus, in September 1962 I left behind the red and yellow school uniform of St Audrey's Infants School and with a group of school friends, now dressed in grey and navy uniforms we crowded into the girls' playground of St Mary's Junior School in Ely's Silver Street. The school had been built with separate entrances and playgrounds for boys and girls and these were still in use. Girls and boys never played together or entered or exited by the same school gates. Games lessons were all separate for boys and girls too. A teacher with a clipboard read out a list of girls who would be in 1A, and twenty or so of us were marched off to Miss Butcher's classroom where we were joined by an equivalent group of boys. We were told we were there because we could already read, and were given hymnbooks. The children in 1B and 1C would not get their own hymnbooks until they could read and some would never reach the required standard. On that first day it was instilled in us that we were the privileged group who had a chance, if we worked hard, to go to the grammar schools. Only later did I discover that my friends had been allocated in 1B and 1C where, to quote a teacher, they would not have 'a hope in hell' of going anywhere other than the local secondary modern. This was in the bitter winter of 1962-63 which was the coldest UK winters since 1740 with blizzards, snow drifts, temperatures as low as -20° C from Christmas onwards and deep snow on the ground until March. The free milk we were given every day sat outside the classroom doors in crates as we entered the playgrounds in the mornings with ice popping out of the tops of the bottles and with the little foil caps perched on top. The forty-four children in IA would become 2As, and then 3As, when the whole year group decamped to another building about half a mile away in Broad Street opposite the entrance to Cherry Hill Park in a school building with mobile huts at the back. In 4A we would devote ourselves week in week out to working on Eleven Plus 'past papers' until we were as adept as possible at intelligence tests, conceptual puzzles, and verbal reasoning. I do not remember any standard maths and English tests.

Throughout my years at Silver Street School, as we called it, the only light relief came from a series of BBC curriculum broadcasts which we listened to live – because schools did not have the equipment to record programmes then – for science, PE and Singing Together, a firm favourite with the whole class and an opportunity to learn and belt out English, Scottish, Welsh and Irish folk songs. School assemblies were never memorable other than when we went to St Mary's or St Peter's Churches which were very near the two school buildings and where assemblies were taken by the local vicars. There was a school trip for those in the fourth year (what is now Y6) which was alternatively a trip to the Royal Tournament, an annual military tattoo that took place at Earl's Court each year, or a visit to the Tower of London and Kew Gardens plus a river trip between the two. I was lucky in that our year went to the latter. Physical punishments were normal but mostly for the boys who were regularly hit by the class teacher with a ruler to the hands delivered at the front of the classroom so the occasion was as much about the humiliation as the punishment. More discreet were the canings which were reserved for behavioural issues, usually fighting at playtime, or spying on the girls' toilets which were located between the two playgrounds so it was possible to climb up from the boys' cubicles to look down on the girls'. In such cases the culprits were sent to the Headmaster's office for caning.

To our family's surprise, and to the great embarrassment of my mother who was never one to 'put on airs', I 'passed' the Eleven Plus at the first go. (There were a further two opportunities to 'get through' via another test, and an interview). I was offered a place at the Ely High School for Girls starting there in September 1966. About 40% – about eight girls and eight boys – of the class of forty-four was selected to go to either the Boys' Grammar School in nearby Soham or the Girls' High School by then located in a new building, opened in 1957, on that 33-acre new educational campus that included St Audrey's Infant school. There we would be reunited with friends who had gone to the private junior school in the city and who possibly had had a better chance of progression there. In addition girls came in on buses from all the Isle of Ely villages: Soham, Witchford and Littleport. The rest of 4A along with all those in 4B and 4C would go to Needham's, the secondary modern school. As children we had no idea what the impact of these decisions made by the Local Authority would have on all our lives.

A formal offer letter arrived from Ely High School but my parents initially assumed it must be a mistake which would be righted in due course. My mother warned me not to tell anyone about it until we were sure the letter had been sent to the right child. There followed a series of communications with a folded yellow card with all the school rules, a long list of uniform requirements which could only be purchased at a shop called Elizabeth's in a road called the Buttermarket in the centre of Ely. These were very precise requirements including a navy blue A-line skirt with six gores, a white blouse and blue and yellow school tie, beret, straw boater and summer gingham dresses in blue, yellow or green for which the size of the gingham squares must be no more than a quarter than an inch. We had to buy both outdoor and indoor shoes, hockey boots and plimsolls, which could only be purchased at Legge's of Ely, the local shoe shop in the High Street. I do not remember any discussions about the cost of these items but I know that no one in our family had ever been shopping before and come away with so many items for one person. In retrospect kitting me out for grammar school must have represented a severe blow to our household finances, and probably to many of the working class families whose daughters had been chosen for a grammar school education.

The school itself had been built in 1957, just nine years before. It was impressively modern with shiny parquet floors and a strong smell of floor polish. Windows were floor to ceiling on one side and there were science labs, art rooms, a library, gym, and special rooms for domestic science and needlework. There was a new headteacher, Eileen Moody, who joined at the same time as the class of 1966, and was very keen on French. She had the cookery and needlework rooms stripped out as soon as she could and replaced them with language laboratories so that girls would aspire to something beyond domestic duties. I only had three cookery lessons where I made a quiche lorraine, and jam tarts and in the third lesson we were taught how to clean an oven. There was what seemed like an enormous school hall, and a 'crush room' where school lunches – all cooked on site – were served, and where girls from the local villages congregated at the end of each day to wait for their buses. Every morning each class had to march into assembly – where the music teacher, Miss Greenwood, always played us in and out with a Mozart piano sonata – past the Deputy Head, Mrs Jones, who would check that everyone was in correct uniform, and if necessary require us to kneel on the ground so that the length of our skirts could be checked with a ruler to ensure they were neither too short nor too long. They were almost always too short because it was now the mid-sixties and mini-skirts were the fashion. Fearing our mothers' anger if we were sent home and required to replace skirts we rolled over the waistlines to achieve the mini-skirt effect which had the advantage that we were able to unroll the waistbands for the daily march-past the deputy head.

Our teachers were all women, although towards the end of the fifth form a few male teachers joined. At the end of the first year, the Lower Three, those who excelled in maths were able to take Latin, so not me. The French sets were divided into those who would benefit from a formal approach (not me either), and those who would use the new language labs and the new audio-visual approach. For French we had new text-books, and sat in individual booths where we were drilled in conversational French, the teacher listening in from her control desk at the front with the technology as new to her as to us. This was an entirely new environment for me. Beyond the curriculum there were music lessons (I took up the clarinet, and already had piano lessons), orchestras and choirs, drama classes, art lessons and occasional trips to other schools on Saturdays for sports fixtures (I was a reserve for hockey until the time came to get a Saturday job), arts activities (I remember a 'day of dance' in Cambridge where schools from across the county of Cambridgeshire took part), languages exchanges, and theatre trips.

Although a grammar school, Ely High School was part of the Village College ethos that was part of all Cambridgeshire education at that time: schools which played a role in their communities and encouraged adult education and social activities to take place in their buildings and for activities like music, sport and drama to work across schools in the county. As a grammar school we competed with public schools and even on one occasion the schools on the American army bases in Lakenheath and Mildenhall for a debating competition. We never mixed with the students at the secondary modern school which moved onto the same site at the time, or with the neighbouring Village Colleges, and contact with the Boys' Grammar School was limited to school plays where girls were needed.

For science we wore navy blue wrap-over science overalls and sat on high stools at benches which all had water taps and gas outlets for Bunsen burners. For hockey we wore what was then known as 'divided skirts' but were actually navy-blue culottes, with white shirts and knitted yellow sweaters and long socks. For netball red legs were the thing because we wore only our t-shirts and knickers. There were regular inspections to ensure that all girls were wearing both regulation white knickers with navy blue knickers on top.

The grammar schools had been set up after the second world war following the 1944 Education Act which proposed three types of secondary school: grammar, technical and secondary modern for which children would be assessed by the Eleven-plus examination. In practice few counties created technical schools but a few, including Kent, did. From the mid-sixties, under Harold Wilson's Labour Government (1964-1970), local authorities who controlled all schools at the time were instructed to prepare for making all their schools 'comprehensive', that is non-selective and abandoning the Eleven-plus. (The news came in 'Circular 10/65'.) Cambridgeshire schools were being threatened with re-organisation throughout my time at Ely High School. My father had come to the view that too many working-class children were being offered places at grammar schools and middle-class families felt that their only alternative was to pay for private education when their children 'failed'. Although Margaret Thatcher as Education Minister reversed the decision, Cambridgeshire was, by then, too far down the track with plans to merge the grammar and secondary education systems. In 1972 our building became a sixth-form college combining the sixth forms of the two grammar schools, and the 11-16 schools were all merged to make comprehensive schools. We became co-educational. Uniforms were abandoned. Male teachers took the head of department roles, and the women teachers the deputies from Principal and across all the subject departments and nobody thought that this was strange, or unfair.

CHAPTER 3

My Mother's family

My mother died in September 2006. She was eighty-one, had been ill for just over a week, and had been taken from Ely to Addenbrooke's Hospital in Cambridge. She had been a widow for almost exactly twenty years and for the last eight years had lived in the centre of Ely in one of eleven alms-houses that make up Thomas Parsons' Square, located next to Cromwell's House in St Mary's Street. The charity that owned the houses had been set up according to the will of Thomas Parsons, a wealthy Ely resident who had died in the 1490s. In the 1840s the governors had commissioned George Basevi, who was the architect for the Fitzwilliam Museum in Cambridge, to build the square of alms-houses near St Mary's Church and Oliver Cromwell's house for local people. My mother had lived most of her life in Ely, and all of it within three miles of the City. She had always lived in rented property and when an opening came to rent one of the tiny single storey houses in Thomas Parsons Square she jumped at the opportunity.

She was born in April 1925 in Prickwillow, three miles from Ely. Her father was a horse keeper and her mother a housewife. There were two older boys, Albert and Leslie. Another daughter,

Phyllis, had been born in 1916 but had died, aged four, in an accident in which paraffin had spilled onto an open fire. My mother never mentioned the incident. Another son, Douglas, would be born six years later. King George V was the reigning monarch and the future Queen Elizabeth II would be born the following year, in April 1926.

Prickwillow was and is a small village – today it has about 400 residents and its landmark buildings, the school (built in 1862), St Peter's Church (1866) and the Post Office which my mother would have known, are all now privately owned. In 1842 a steam drainage pump was installed in what is today a small museum of drainage.

Prickwillow was once located on the Great River Ouse but this changed in 1829-20 when improvements following the Bedford Level Drainage Act of 1827:

> *'the Rivers Ouze (sic) and Lark …are much grown up and obstructed by mud, soil and rubbish …it is necessary to scour out, cleanse and deepen the same … and to straighten and otherwise improve the said Rivers Ouze and Lark, by conveying the waters of the said River Ouze into, through or near a certain Cut called Sandy's or Sandal's Cut…by altering or abandoning part of the present line of the said River Ouze below a place called Prickwillow.'*

The Great Ouse was moved north of Ely leaving Prickwillow on the banks of the River Lark as it is today. The Victorian village was built on the river bed of the Great Ouse, on the 'roddam' or 'rodham', the silted dried river bed that is much more robust for building than the nearby shrinking peat. Like much of the Burnt Fen area, Prickwillow lies below sea level and is only viable if excess water is pumped away. In the eighteenth century this was done using windmills but throughout the nineteenth and twentieth centuries steam, diesel and electricial pumps were introduced. Information and working pumps can be seen today at Prickwillow's Drainage Museum. A steam engine was installed by the River Lark first in 1831 which was replaced in the 1880s, and in 1924 a diesel engine replaced steam and remained in use until the 1970s when an automatic electrical pump was introduced.

I had seen my mother in hospital the day before she died and planned to see her the next day but on the day itself I was on my way from London to a work event in Leeds and on the train from London Kings' Cross with a colleague when the call came through to my mobile from the ward to say, 'You should come at once'. We had just left Stevenage so I determined to get off at the next station wherever it might be and, as luck would have it, it was Grantham in Lincolnshire, the birthplace, just six months after my mother in 1925, of Margaret Thatcher, the UK's first female Prime Minister, and without doubt the living individual towards whom my mother felt the greatest animosity. I jumped off the train as soon as it stopped at Grantham Station. 'How do I get to Cambridge?' I asked the railway man on the platform. 'Your train is right there, Miss', he said, pointing to a train sitting at one of the other platforms, 'Change at Ely'. Margaret Thatcher was on my mind briefly – I remembered her as Education Secretary in the 1970s when I was a student at Ely High School for Girls, a girls' grammar school, and when all the talk in the town had been of our school being forced to become a comprehensive school. On arrival in post as Education Secretary Margaret Thatcher halted all such plans, and then became famous as the Secretary of State who abolished free milk for 7-11 year olds – I had hated having to drink the free milk every day at junior school – and became known as 'Margaret Thatcher, Milk Snatcher'. My parents had hated the Edward Heath government (1970- 1974) of which she was part,

PRICKWILLOW TODAY WITH ITS WAR MEMORIAL (LEFT) AND HOUSES BELOW THE LEVEL OF THE ROAD

who had capped public sector workers' pay when inflation was rising. They supported the miners' actions in cutting overtime, even in the face of the Three-day week which Edward Heath put in place in January 1974, leaving households across the country with no electricity, their evenings spent in candlelight. Margaret Thatcher's arrival in Government in 1979 signalled for them full-on class warfare with the Government determined to take on the miners, increase taxes, shrink the public sector, 'rolling back the frontiers of socialism', and talking of 'the enemy within' which was widely interpreted in our family as referring to the working class, meaning us.

The Peterborough to Ely railway line

My journey that September day to Cambridge took me first to Ely, via Peterborough and Whittlesey. At the time I did not know that my mother's male ancestors had worked for decades on that particular line of railway track. All my ancestors, except one were born in the Isle of Ely. Allen Owen, the only person in my entire family history who did not originate in the Cambridgeshire Fens, was born in the Cheadle area near Manchester in 1824. He had travelled from the North-west of England in 1847, to work for the Eastern Counties Railway (ECR) and worked as a platelayer, or track maintenance worker, for the rest of his life until his death in 1880 at the age of fifty-six. His son, my mother's grandfather, William Owen, had been born lame, and as a boy worked as an agricultural labourer. When newly married in the early 1880s he secured a job and a tied cottage as a gatekeeper and pointsman for ECR on the Whittlesey Road from March and he spent all his working life there living in a cottage railway line where my grandmother grew up. I almost certainly passed his house and his railway gates on my way towards Ely that day but it is impossible to locate where the house was today.

The railway developments of the 1840s

Allen Owen had grown up in modest circumstances in the North-west of England. His father was a weaver and his mother Ann Allen was from Ireland. At the age of twelve Allen Owen joined the household of a local farmer as a house servant in what was then a hamlet called Gill Bent in the parish of Cheadle in the county of Chester. The hamlet was home to a few farmers and their agricultural workers. Allen Owen's parents had married in Manchester Cathedral in 1822 (actually, it did not become a Cathedral until 1847), where his father, Samuel Owen, had been baptised twenty years before. They had a daughter and Allen Owen was their only son and, I assume, he was named after his mother. Things changed for Allen Owen in the 1840s when the second wave of railway building started in England and the countryside around him began to change because of the new railway developments. He was probably ambitious for a better life and because he was getting into his late teens his time as a house servant was nearing its end and the next step for him would have been to become a farm labourer. He was a single man and when local railway companies put calls out for labourers he signed up to be a navvy with the possibility of earning more money and creating a better future for himself. A station and line were built at Cheadle but the original plan must have been thought inadequate because soon after in 1845, a further line from Stafford to Manchester was built and the Cheadle station was closed down and a new station built to accommodate the junction of the two lines at Cheadle Hulme. These developments meant that at the age of twenty-one Allen Owen was taken on as a railway labourer earning between 11 and 14p per ten-hour day, working six days per week, digging out the soil and laying down the railway tracks, building the embankments by hand with minimal equipment beyond a pick and shovel and possibly some explosives. He would have lived by the tracks in make-shift huts in shanty towns alongside other navvies moving along the line as work progressed. The pressure to complete the lines on time, the long hours and the hard nature of the work blasting through tunnels and laying tracks, made for a quicker, if more dangerous, way to make a reasonable income than poorly paid agricultural work. The railway contractors needed men fast and were often up against time to complete their contracts so when they found reliable hard-working men they kept in touch and called on them when new contracts came in even if they were many miles away and in another part of the country.

Migration to the Fens in the late 1840s

Allen Owen met several fellow workers of about the same age on the Cheadle railway project and by 1851 a group of them had all relocated to Oldeamere near Whittlesey, working on the very line that I was travelling on the day of my mother's death. It was an interesting time for them to arrive in the Whittlesey area, about six miles east of Peterborough and on the northern edge of Cambridgeshire. The drainage projects of the seventeenth century had changed the Fenland landscape into agricultural land but one of the final drainage projects in the area, the draining of Whittlesey Mere, was still outstanding. It was one of the last and largest big inland lakes to be drained, being about three miles by six in size. Along with the building of the railways its disappearance at the time when Allen Owen was settling nearby was seen as another of symbol of the Victorian innovation. The Mere was on the itinerary of the extraordinary 'Voyage Round the Fens' by Lord Orford (George Walpole, 1730-1791), known as a playboy and a rake, in July and August 1774: this was a cruise around the area by a fleet of river barges. The pleasure trip route followed the Rive Nene, through Outwell and Upwell to Whittlesey Mere to which the party returned on several occasions because of the fine fishing and partying. From the account of the voyage it seems that the Mere had been a rich source of fish and wildfowl, and of sedge, reed and peat before drainage as well as a popular place in winter for ice skating and fairs. The drainage project was funded by a group of local landowners and turned the Mere into farmland in the early 1850s.

Allen Owen, his friends and their families settled into Eastern Counties Railway cottages in Oldeamere to the east of Whittlesey in an area between the River Nene and the Twenty Foot river, a drainage channel. The name Oldeamere, meaning 'lake by the old river', suggests that it too was on the site of a drained mere. The railway line opened in 1847, which is when the men seem to have travelled south suggesting that they probably came down to work long-term for Eastern Counties Railway maintaining the network as platelayers rather than as navvies building the lines. One of

My Mother's family

ALLEN AND ELIZA OWEN'S GRAVESTONE IN COATES CHURCHYARD

Allen Owen's friends, Samuel Mottram, had married in Cheadle and settled with his wife in Oldeamere. The Mottrams took in Allen Owen, by then 27 and still single, and another younger worker, Ben Penny, as lodgers. Mottram, Owen and Penny were all ECR railway workers. Next door was Thomas Mounfield and his wife and family, also from Cheadle, and there was another neighbour, Harry Barker, from Staffordshire. All five men had been employed together in the North-west, and were now settled in Cambridgeshire.

Owen in 1851 married Eliza Hewson, a young local woman nine years his junior. Although they lived in Oldeamere they were married in St Mary's Church in Whittlesey as there were no nearer churches at the time. They had five children between 1855 and 1865, two girls and three boys: William, my great-grandfather, was their eldest son. Navvies had a reputation for hard living and drinking and there is at least one reference to Allen Owen in the local news, the *Cambridge Chronicle*, when in September 1870 he was involved in an affray with a neighbour and fellow railway labourer, John Hudson, which resulted in Hudson being convicted of assault and being forced to pay a fine of 2s 6d and legal costs of 17s 9d. Allen Owen died ten years after the incident at the age of 54 years in 1880. Eliza Owen survived into her seventies and died nearly thirty years later in 1907. She was buried alongside her husband and a gravestone stands in the churchyard of Holy Trinity Parish Church in Coates suggesting that by then she had the means to afford a decent burial and stone.

Travelling from Peterborough to Whittlesey in September 2006 I was suddenly aware again of the familiarity and flatness of the land, the large expanses of farmland divided not by hedges, stone walls or fences but by dead-straight drains, ditches and dykes which were vital in taking away the water from the soil, directing it towards the cut-off channels for pumping up to the rivers. Travelling from Lincolnshire to Ely and then onto Cambridge the land become darker and flatter, with fewer trees and houses.

A childhood in the fens

I have lived away from the Fens for most of my life and I've rarely met people outside the area who come from the Isle of Ely. When I'm asked where I'm from I've usually been met with blank faces. Some clarification is usually necessary – the Fens perhaps, or East

Cambridgeshire. Most people know Cambridge and will then nod and say, 'What a lovely place to grow up'. If they have any concept of Ely it will be of its Cathedral. Some will have been to the cathedral as a visitor on a day trip, perhaps when they were 'at Cambridge'. Not many will have stayed the night. Even today the idea that Ely is a city surprises people.

As my train pulled into Ely the cathedral came into view in the familiar way it had done every time I had returned to Ely by road or rail over the years, suddenly appearing, as a huge building isolated but dominating the vast black land around it. Waiting for my connection for Cambridge I thought about how different the landscape would have been before the big drainage projects of the seventeenth century, with local men making a living through fishing and fowling, pasturing cattle and moving round the flooded lands on stilts or in flat-bottomed punts.

My mother died later that day. Her life spanned the massive changes of the twentieth century. Born in Prickwillow she had left school at thirteen with no qualifications and started out as a live-in parlour maid at the King's School, Ely, an independent boys' school located in the ecclesiastical buildings immediately surrounding Ely Cathedral. It is sad to see her name in the 1939 War Register where she is an employee, aged thirteen, alongside all the boy students who are the same age or older. She attended confirmation classes organised by the school and was confirmed in Ely Cathedral by the Bishop of Ely the year after her employment began. Like many of my relatives she lived all her life in the Isle of Ely and was, like them, defined by it.

CHAPTER 4

My mother's family

My mother's father, Henry Butcher, was the only grandparent that I knew. (My father's mother, Rachel Dorling, the youngest child of William and Mary Clements, had died in 1949 and, as was the custom, her widower, William Dorling, my grandfather, went to live with one of his daughters, Aunt Flo, who lived in Littleport with her husband Charlie and their eight-year old daughter, Mary. An older sister, Lil, had been widowed in her thirties and was living near Cambridge with her young son and father-in-law but Aunt Flo was nearer. William Dorling died in 1956 and the following year Flo's husband Charlie died at the age of fifty leaving Aunt Flo a widow until her own death at the age of 92 in 1994.)

My mother never spoke about her own mother, Rose Owen Butcher, other than to say that she died on the same day as Ruth Ellis (13th July 1955), the last woman to be hanged in the UK. The death of Ruth Ellis was an important memory for my mother who felt a connection to her and mentioned her more than once, and that Ruth Ellis and my grandmother's lives ended on the same day must have had some significance for her. My mother and Ruth Ellis were both born in the mid-1920s, as were Margaret Thatcher and Elizabeth II, other women that my mother mentioned often

My mother's family

but seldom in a good way. My mother and Ruth Ellis both left school in their early teens without qualifications: Ruth Ellis worked as a waitress, my mother as a parlour maid. Those were the similarities. Ruth Ellis was a young woman from Rhyl in Wales who became a Knightsbridge nightclub manager and got caught up in a turbulent relationship with an upper-class amateur racing driver, David Blakely, and shot him dead when their relationship faltered. In her late teenage years my mother had looked for glamour in the Fens and had gone to dances and flirted with American GIs stationed in local Suffolk airbases during the second world war, splitting from her mother irrevocably because of it. My mother was thirty and in the final stages of pregnancy with me when Ruth Ellis, 28, shot David Blakely outside the Magdala public house in South Hill Park, North London, on Easter Sunday, April 10th, 1955, and I was just under 12 weeks old when Ruth Ellis and my grandmother died on Wednesday, 13 July. The hearing for Ruth Ellis lasted a day and a half, and although she pleaded not guilty because she wanted an opportunity to put her side of the story she confirmed that she had intended to kill David Blakely. The jury took twenty-five minutes to decide that she was guilty. She did not appeal her sentence although many people wanted her to – if successful she would probably have served seven years in prison, been released and quietly forgotten. 'Justice' was swift and she was executed in Holloway Prison after only three weeks and two days in the condemned suite.

Although my grandmother was well until heart failure killed her suddenly at the age of sixty-eight I do not think she ever saw me. My mother and grandmother had not been reconciled when my mother was in a Cambridge hospital for many months in her late teens following an industrial accident at the Ely Jam Factory where she worked during the second world war – a fact my uncle revealed in the funeral car on the day of my mother's burial in

2006 – nor did my grandmother attend my parents' wedding in 1948, although my grandfather and her brothers did. I doubt whether my mother attended her mother's funeral. We had no photographs of my grandmother, nor evidence of her existence. Beyond that one comment about the date of her death she was never mentioned including by my mother's three brothers when they came to visit, although one uncle told me subsequently that my grandmother was a lovely woman and that when my mother started to go dancing with Americans their mother issued an ultimatum forcing a choice between the Americans and her family.

My mother was very conscious of what she considered her poor background. She judged my father's family to be more respectable because my father's older sister and brother, Flo and Wag, both owned their own houses and another sister's husband was a carpenter, a skilled worker. Her brothers were unskilled labourers. My maternal grandfather came from Mildenhall in West Suffolk, the far reaches of Burnt Fen, and had been a horse-keeper all his life. The family moved around from farm to farm following work, living in tied cottages, at a time when heavy horses were fast being replaced by farm machinery. Henry Butcher would have worked long hours looking after the animals and stables, ensuring that the horses were fed and fit to work and then supervising them during the working day. For someone responsible for animals there would have been very few days off. The houses my grandparents lived in would have been basic with few facilities: no running water, electricity or domestic appliances. My mother once took me to an elderly aunt's house on a farm near Whittlesey and warned me in advance not to mention the absence of water and electricity although I was too young to understand the implications of what she was saying. My grandmother must have had the ability to run a household on very few resources, a skill inherited by my mother. Although we must have been poor when I was a child it didn't feel so and we always seemed to have what we needed because of my mother's careful eye on income and expenditure, a sharp eye for opportunities to save or make money and by what we would now call 'managing expectations'.

My maternal grandfather would have been very aware from the 1940s onwards that horse-keeping was becoming a thing of the past as motorised farm vehicles became more prevalent and that there was no point in encouraging his sons to follow suit. The next generation were more interested in cars, vans and motor-bikes. Henry's father, Jacob Butcher, had also been a horse-keeper and whereas his brothers – the 1911 census records that Henry's mother had had nineteen live births between 1875 and 1904, with eleven children surviving at the time of the census – seem to have moved straight into agricultural labouring, Henry was singled out to follow his father into horse-keeping. My uncle told me that his father was a gentle man with a real affinity to animals and particularly heavy horses. He worked with all breeds including the famous chestnut, or sorrel, Suffolk Punches. Insofar as I remember him at all it is of an old man sitting on a stepladder in our back yard, not speaking but quietly smoking a pipe. Both my parents had strong early memories of agricultural work with horses and traction engines, and throughout my childhood a family treat for the three of us was to go to county shows to see heavy horses, traction engines and fairground organs. When my father bought us a second-hand record-player in the early 1960s it came with a few LPs – *Cliff Sings* from 1959 I remember particularly – but he started two collections, one of fairground organ music and the other of country music which became our regular listening at weekends.

Henry Butcher, my grandfather, was older than his wife Rose by ten years. He was illiterate and signed documents with an X. Rose had come from Whittlesey, in the north of the Isle of Ely,

HENRY BUTCHER, MY GRANDFATHER

and had been a maid in several local upper middle-class families for over a decade before getting married. It was an odd match. I realised later, when writing this memoir, that Rose's own family in Whittlesey were not farm labourers and not at all what my mother imagined, but Rose's father, William Owen, had died in 1917, before my mother was born and his wife, Elizabeth, had married again in her mid-sixties, this time to a farm labourer. This presumably gave my mother the impression that her family were farm labourers like my grandfather. Rose's last position before her marriage was as a general domestic servant for a young brother and his sister on a farm in north Suffolk. Rose had already worked as a junior maid for their parents, Stephen and Florence Coxon, in Wisbech and must have been perceived by Florence Coxon as a sensible choice as a servant to accompany her son and daughter who were setting up a farm together in Suffolk. Stephen Coxon Senior was a dentist in Wisbech and Ely, and had had a practice in Cromwell's house, a thirteenth century house in St Mary's Street, Ely, in the 1890s before it became the vicarage for St Mary's Church which was next door (and next door to my mother's last home). Oliver Cromwell (1599-1658) had been left the house in 1636 and lived in Ely for about ten years. After my father died in 1986 my mother and I visited the local vicar there to arrange the funeral but very soon afterwards it was sold to the local council who turned it into a museum celebrating Cromwell's association with the house.

Coxon Senior seems to have been more than a local dentist. At times he had a London practice and was a member of the Odontological Society of Great Britain. He registered patents for several new dental procedures and equipment and later in retirement became mayor of King's Lynn. His wife followed him as mayor becoming King's Lynn's first female mayor. She went on to qualify as a barrister in her seventies. There are sketches of both in the National Portrait Gallery's collection, and portraits of Florence who became quite famous in Norfolk. The son and daughter were in their early twenties when they took on the farm in Fressingfield in the years before the first world war, with Rose Owen, much the same age, as their general servant. Coxon Junior was active in the village socially, a keen supporter of the boy scouts and a recruiter for the army and, as the only domestic servant, Rose must have had to cook and service many formal dinners and gatherings. When the farm was sold in 1913 Rose returned to her parents' home in Coates near Whittlesey, where she stayed during the early months of the First World War. Coxon served in the first world war and then embarked on a diplomatic career overseas but died on board ship returning to the UK from Africa shortly after the war. Florence married a scientist with whom she

THE AUTHOR WITH SHIRE HORSES AT A COUNTY SHOW, AROUND 1960

lived in Myanmar (then Burma) where he took up teaching for the colonial service. Rose must have held her own as general servant to the family as she stayed in their service for several years.

Henry Butcher and Rose Owen married in St John's Church, Whittlesey in 1915, when Henry was already thirty-seven years old and Rose, twenty-seven. They moved to a farm in Burnt Fen near Prickwillow where Henry had employment and went on to have five children, three boys and two girls. Their firstborn, Phyllis, as said already, died at the age of four in a tragic accident with a paraffin heater when their second child, Albert, was just two years old. Two further boys and my mother were born later. No one ever mentioned Phyllis and I only found out about her from a cousin some years after my mother's death.

When my grandmother, Rose Butcher, died in 1955 my grandfather was in his late-seventies and his youngest son, then in his twenties, was living at home. The two of them muddled through in their house in the village of Queen Adelaide on the edges of Ely near Prickwillow for a while but then they both came to live with us. Our terraced house was small with only two proper bedrooms and a tiny room where I slept, which had no electricity and was attached to my parents' bedroom, so the house was cramped but my mother never complained about having two extra men in the house for whom she would have done all the cooking, laundry and housekeeping until my grandfather died in 1960 when I was five, and my uncle moved on.

Whittlesea

There are no photographs of Rose Owen or of her family. I do not know if my mother had any photographs of her own childhood and youth because when she had breast cancer in the early 1990s she destroyed all the photographs she had at the time, leaving me with only a very few that my father had given me before he died.

What did I find about about Rose Elizabeth Owen's family? It was not, as my mother assumed, poorer than my father's relatives. Rose was born in Eastrea, or more precisely in the Eastern Counties Railway cottage on the Whittlesey Road from March in March 1888, and baptised in Holy Trinity Church in Coates six months later. The town of Whittlesey is recorded in the Domesday Book as 'Witesie" and is about seven miles to the east of Peterborough on the Ely-Peterborough railway line. The railways were almost as important as the drainage projects in opening up the Fens and allowing travel between the different places. The 'sey' or 'sea' (the older spelling is Whittlesea) in the name refers to its origin as an 'island' of which there were many in the Fens where different settlements, like Whittlesey, Ely and Coates were built on higher land and less likely to flood than the surrounding land and were, therefore, habitable. 'Whittle' probably refers to the owner of the 'Isle'. Whittlesey is only three miles from Flag Fen which is now a major archaeological project following discoveries, in the early 1980s, of timbers, bones and metal fragments suggesting a Bronze Age settlement. Whittlesey Mere, which before it was drained between 1845 and 1852 was a three-mile by six-mile lake, one of the longest lakes in lowland England, is nearby and is mentioned by John Clare, one of the few writers who were critical of the changes the drainage brought with it, in his poem, *The Shepherd's Calendar*.

> The clouds of starnels dailey fly
> Blackening thro the evening sky
> To whittleseas reed wooded mere
> And ozier holts by rivers near
> And many a mingld swarthy crowd
> Fly too and fro to dreary fen
> Dull winters weary flight agen
> Flopping on heavy wings away
> As soon as morning wakens grey
> And when the sun sets round and red
> Returns to naked woods to bed'
>
> *January – A Winter's Day* by John Clare (1827)

Whittlesey and Coates were built on two adjacent 'islands' in the Fens when much of the land between them was marshy or flooded. In Coates today there are two village greens which are dissected by the main road, the A605 from March to Whittlesey, cutting across agricultural land. If you drive from Ely and March on the Whittlesey Road through Turves and Oldeamere to Coates and then on to Whittlesey via Eastrea you will pass places where different members of Rose Owen's family lived in the nineteenth and twentieth centuries, all originally discrete villages surrounded by land which had been subject to flooding before the area was drained in the seventeenth century. There is an old Wesleyan Church, built in 1840, in the middle of the North Green in Coates which has been converted into a commercial centre and to its left is Holy Trinity Church, the Anglian Church that was built the same year. In 1839 there was a ceremonial laying of the chief corner stone, a sort of 'groundbreaking' event to mark the beginning of construction. There was a parade, hymn-singing and prayers and the event concluded with a dinner at the Falcon Inn in Whittlesey. There were around 600 villagers living in 130 dwellings then, and since then many of my mother's relatives have been buried in the churchyard of Holy Trinity Church in Coates. Most prominent is a double gravestone for Rose Owen's maternal great-grandparents, Ann and John Neal, born in the very early nineteenth century. As a widow Ann Neal ran the Falcon Inn in Whittlesey in the 1860s where the church's inaugural events concluded in 1839.

HOLY TRINITY CHURCH, COATES, TODAY

Whittlesey has two parish churches, St Mary and St Andrew, about 500 metres apart and in the period before the dissolution of the monasteries in the mid-sixteenth century Whittlesey looked two ways ecclesiastically. In medieval times the area was developed by monastic houses (Ely, Thorney, Ramsey, Peterborough and Croyland), with monks and nuns farming the land, draining the Fens and maintaining the waterways. St Mary's, in Whittlesey, which took in Coates and Oldeamere, and St Andrew's each belonged to one of the nearby ancient abbeys of Thorney and Ely. In 1849 Whittlesey was absorbed within the Diocese of Ely. Although the churches of St Mary, Whittlesey and Coates were connected ecclesiastically, administratively Whittlesey St Andrew took in the local villages of Coates, Eastrea, Oldeamere, Pondersbridge and Turves.

The Neals of Turves

In the mid-nineteenth century Coates was a farming community and most of the men there were farmers or farm labourers and their families, with other individuals servicing the agricultural economy in occupations such as wheelwrights, shepherds and blacksmiths. Although my great-great-great grandfather, John Neal, had started out as an agricultural labourer in Coates, by 1851 he was farming fourteen acres in the nearby village of Turves as well as running a public house, the Three Horseshoes in Turves, where he lived with his wife Ann, their five children and a live-in servant. Much augmented, the pub is still there today by the railway line. Ten years later their son and two daughters had married and the son, Thomas Neal, died shortly after his marriage at the age of twenty-two leaving a widow with a young child. In 1855 John Neal made the local news when he was charged with short-selling and using 'deficit measures'. He died in 1866 at the age of sixty-one and we know he left money to his wife Ann, probably around £280 which

My mother's family

THE THREE HORSESHOES IN TURVES TODAY

at today's prices would be around £10,000 and certainly enough for her to buy into the Falcon Inn, a large eighteenth century coaching house in the heart of Whittlesey, where she became the landlady. Five months after John Neal's death, their daughter, Rebecca Neal (my great-great grandmother), then in her late twenties, was herself widowed and left with four young children, including my mother's grandmother, Elizabeth Barrett.

Rebecca Neal had married well. Her young husband, James Barrett, had been farming 18 acres before his death and his family owned much of the farmland around Quaker's Drove in Coates. Her in-laws, the Barretts, were Calvinist Baptists and may have disapproved of the marriage, particularly as Rebecca was pregnant at the time of the wedding. The farmland and any assets seem to have been reclaimed by the Barrett family on their son's death as Rebecca Barrett had to leave the farm and had very little money of her own although her youngest child, a boy called George, seems to have inherited his father's share in adulthood. All four children were under six years old when their father died. (In a similar

THE FALCON IN WHITTLESEY

predicament Rebecca Barrett's sister-in-law, the young widow of Thomas Barrett, had left her young daughter with her parents in Coates and moved permanently to London where she worked for the rest of her life as a bell maid in the Charing Cross Hotel in the Strand, marrying again in her late thirties. She hardly saw her daughter as a child but the daughter moved to London.)

The option of leaving four young children in Coates with her mother who was running the Falcon Inn on her own, was presumably out of the question and it must have seemed sensible for Rebecca Barrett to move in with her widowed mother, Ann Neal, at the Falcon Inn. Her sister and brother-in-law lived next door.

The Falcon Inn housed Ann Neal as landlady, her daughter Rebecca Barrett who probably helped with running the establishment, the four young children and a servant. Whatever the Barrett children's early lives were like living at The Falcon Inn, it seems that by 1877 there was some pressure on the older girls to leave home as both Elizabeth and her sister Ann married when

JOHN AND ANN NEAL'S GRAVESTONE IN HOLY TRINITY CHURCHYARD IN COATES

only sixteen and seventeen in July and October that year (in Holy Trinity Church at Coates). Perhaps their grandmother, Ann Neal, by now in her mid-seventies had had to give up the Falcon Inn for some reason, possibly ill-health. She died two years later and there seems to have been enough money for a substantial gravestone but at that point Rebecca Barrett, again with few resources, was forced to take lodgings with a local agricultural worker, Cornelius Thompson, back in Coates and to survive financially, she and her two younger children, then in their early teens, were all working on the land as agricultural workers. Rebecca Barrett always considered herself to be a boarder in Thompson's house but in her mid-forties she had another daughter who when baptised at Holy Trinity, Coates is described in the Parish Records as 'Barrett, Susan Ann Thompson dau. of Cornelius Thompson (supposed) and Rebecca Barrett, widow of Coates, b. 30 June 1884.'

Elizabeth Barrett, Rebecca Barrett's daughter, was the mother of my grandmother, Rose Owen, who, as said before, was born in 1888, eleven years after William and Elizabeth Barrett Owen's wedding. Her brothers, William and George were ten and five and her parents had already lost three children as babies. Of William and Elizabeth Owen's twelve children only Rose and three brothers survived into adult life.

Stuntney, 1915

In 1915 at the age of twenty-seven Rose Owen married my grandfather in North Witchford. My grandfather looked after shire horses on Wade's Farm, just off the Stuntney Causeway, one of the original access roads to Ely when the two places were otherwise divided by water, and about two miles south of Ely railway station. Rose Owen moved from living as a servant at the comfortable homes of the Coxons in Wisbech and Suffolk, part of a middle-class well-connected household, to living in a labourer's cottage in the Fens with a husband ten years older who could neither read nor write. Wades Farm was one of the biggest farming operations in Cambridgeshire when my mother was growing up and one of the first to replace its horses with tractors. In the 1930s my grandfather would have been struggling to stay in employment as a horse-keeper as tractors were taking over everywhere. At the time Wade's Farm owned a farmhouse, significant farm buildings and two labourers' cottages including the one where my grandparents lived. My grandfather had a good rapport with horses and great patience in dealing with them. When he moved on to another farm in the 1930s he worked with the slightly smaller Suffolk Punch chestnut-coloured horses at a farm in Padnal Fen near Prickwillow.

CHAPTER 5

The Americans Arrive

Black Horse Drove 1884

It is easy to find my paternal great great-grandmother, Rhoda Francis Clements (1801-1884), on genealogy websites online, which is remarkable for a woman who lived an obscure life in rural Cambridgeshire and was officially a pauper when she died in late 1884, in a tiny hamlet called Black Horse Drove in the north of the county near the Norfolk border. Black Horse Drive had only two hundred residents at the time, about the same as now. She was living there with her son Robert Clements and his wife Eliza and would certainly have died at home, as was the custom in a time before the National Health Service. She had lived a long life and was eighty-three years old when she died.

The population of Black Horse Drove, three miles north of Littleport and off Ten Mile Bank, the main road along the bank of the River Ouse towards Norfolk, was made up of a few farmers, a school mistress, a publican, a platelayer or railway worker with the rest agricultural labourers and their families. Robert Clements was one of the agricultural workers, and that his wife, Eliza Clements, was not working suggests that by then Robert's income could keep the three of them. He was in his late fifties at the time. We know that he could sign his name, and could probably read and write, because he was a witness to his mother's second marriage in 1866, and after Rhoda Clements' death his circumstances improved briefly because in 1891, at the age of sixty-four he was a grocer, and the couple had both a young female servant and a boarder, a man who was working locally on the land. It is hard to see how he managed to save enough money to set himself up as a grocer but he seems to have had some livestock and presumably a shop in the front of his house. Running a business did not suit him and in January 1898 he was up before the courts for bankruptcy, owing £23 even after having sold a sow, five pigs and some potatoes. Following the hearing, his position possibly worse than before, Robert Clements, by now seventy with a wife six years older and not able to retire, was forced back on the land as an agricultural worker again.

His wife, Eliza, had been widowed at the age of twenty-six and had three daughters from her first marriage. She married Robert who was five years younger in December 1849. The couple had a daughter together, and four boys who all died in infancy.

Black Horse Drove is still there today, a tiny village which lies about six feet below sea level and which would have been marked out as a drove to provide a route through the Fen at the time when the area was drained. The Fens still have a large number of roads called 'droves' which were the main routes across the Fens until the Second World War, when providing food in the Fens became an essential part of the war effort and there was a sudden imperative to concrete over the droves to create passable roads. Until then droves could be out of action when muddy and constantly in need of improvements. The droves had been created as access roads to reclaimed agricultural lands and have retained the name. Originally kept in the ownership of the Enclosure or Drainage Commissioners, they have, over time, become part of the public road system.

Born Rhoda Francis, my great great-grandmother had been widowed a second time in 1875, following nine years of marriage to James Haylock Boatright, a farm labourer with whom she lived in Soham Fen, about fourteen miles from Black Horse Drove. James Boatright had also been widowed and had had a period of itinerant farm-working across the wider Fenland area, most recently in Lincolnshire where he boarded for a few years before settling down in a late second marriage with Rhoda Clements. After his death she must have had some dealings with St Mary's Parish in Ely because she was formally declared a pauper but she escaped the Ely workhouse by going to live with her son and his wife in Black Horse Drove.

Ely 1960

I remember exactly when I first heard about Rhoda Francis Clements and saw her photograph because in 1960 when I was five years old my parents were contacted out-of-the-blue by a retired American civil servant who was researching her family history. As an only child I was included in all that went on in our house even from a very young age – from the age of eleven when I passed the Eleven Plus exam my father put me in charge of any formal correspondence – and the existence of Ina Clements was an exciting revelation to the whole family. Ina Clements wrote to say that she wanted to make contact with her distant English relatives and to see the village her father, Samuel Clements Junior, Rhoda's grandson by her fourth child, also called Samuel, had left as a small boy in the mid-nineteenth century. Ina Clements was a single woman in her early seventies by this time, quite elegant – my mother called her 'stately', approvingly – and she had grown up and been educated in Kansas, Missouri, from where she had gone to Washington D.C. for a career as an 'auditor of the public health service records of commissioned officers in the U.S.

military'. No one here knew what that involved as my family had little experience of people in office jobs – something that became an issue for me when as a teenager I needed a passport because we could not think of anyone in the approved categories we could ask to provide a countersignature for the application – and indeed I do not know whether my father or his sisters were aware of any American connection in the family until Ina Clements' first blue aerogram arrived. My father's parents had died some years before and there was no one left from their generation to ask. This was before English people bothered with family history and my parents and aunts were bemused by being contacted, but nevertheless agreed to gather to meet Ina Clements at our small terraced house in Ely. The thin foldable airmail letters became familiar because, after her visit, Ina shared her findings with her wider family and more American relatives started to write to us and some came to visit. Ina Clements herself never came back but stayed in contact until she died.

In the photograph that Ina brought with her Rhoda is a small woman, seated and dressed all in black with flat dark hair like mine parted in the centre under a black bonnet with a white ribbon. She is staring out at the camera whilst leaning on a table, a Bible in her right hand. Ina Clements had the photograph made from an old tin-type, and the original must have been taken in Ely sometime after the death of Rhoda's first husband, my great great-grandfather John Clements who died in October 1861, but before the death of their son Samuel Clements, Ina's grandfather, who originally owned the photograph.

Samuel Clements died of inflammation of the lungs at the age of thirty-seven in Danville, Kentucky in January 1863 where he was involved in the American Civil War, having been recruited in Illinois where he settled. After his death Samuel's widow, Mary Clements, moved the family on from Illinois to Kansas. It is possible the photograph was taken for Mary Clements, Samuel Clements Senior's wife, to take with her when she left their home village of Prickwillow in Cambridgeshire for America in 1857 to join her husband, but it is unlikely as John Clements was still alive then and would certainly have been part of the photograph too. We know from Samuel Clements' army records that he was literate – I have seen the text of his last letter to his wife from the army hospital – so he probably wrote to Rhoda requesting the photograph when he heard of the death of his father, possibly many months after the event itself as news would have travelled slowly. I am sure she would have asked her son Robert to read the letter to her: most official records from my father's family up until the twentieth century are signed with an X and I doubt that Rhoda herself could read.

The Prickwillow census records for 1861 were destroyed during flooding so although we can see where Rhoda Clements' older children were living we do not know exactly what Rhoda Francis Clements' own circumstances were in her early widow-hood, but we do know that only two of the twelve children she had with John Clements were living at home with her at the time. The older of the two boys at home, Job Clements, was seventeen and had been working as an agricultural labourer for at least four years by this time, enabling Rhoda Clements to stay on in one of the labourers' cottages along the bank of the River Lark where she had lived all her married life. The Lark is one of three tributaries of the Great Ouse river that mark out the area where my ancestors lived along with the Little Ouse and the Wissey. (The Great Ouse, the fifth longest river in the UK, has been re-routed several times since the thirteenth century as part of successive attempts to drain off the area, or to deal with flooding. Its best known tributary is the Cam.)

There is a road on either side of the stretch off the River Lark between Prickwillow and its confluence with the Great Ouse south

RHODA FRANCIS CLEMENTS

of Littleport with Branch Bank along one side and Padnal Bank on the other. Rhoda and John Clements lived on the Branch Bank side. Even today there are only a few houses along that road and they are widely spaced. The Fen in Prickwillow was not really suitable for building as houses would sink unless built on piles. Behind the houses today the flat black agricultural land stretches out as far as the eye can see with an occasional tree but not much else – just vast fields with black peat soil. If you look towards Ely the cathedral is almost always visible in the distance. Rhoda and John Clements moved there shortly after the first steam pumping engines were in place sometime after 1819. To have the photograph taken she would have walked with her youngest son Richard, twelve at the time, the three miles to Ely and back, probably on a Saturday or Thursday which were market days and when people from the villages would have travelled in, to the photographer's studio – perhaps Samuel Clements had sent money from America to cover all the costs – and then again to Ely to collect it and perhaps back again to Ely for posting at the Post Office in the Market Place which was established in the mid-1850s.

Over most of my childhood my parents would be contacted by American relations who were planning holidays in England and who wanted to make the diversion to the Fens to see where their ancestors came from. It was always a bit of a mystery to me to understand what they got from the visits as there seemed little of interest in the flat black peat soil and the long stretches of agricultural land that surrounded Ely for many miles. There was even a dearth of footpaths, trees or bushes because the agricultural land was considered so precious that farmers resisted any roadside developments that would compromise the space available for crops. Instead the fields were delineated by dykes and ditches and one memory I have from my childhood is of news of fatal accidents when newly-qualified drivers, often still in their teens, would miscalculate a corner along one of the fen roads late at night and literally 'die in a ditch'. My parents had never had a holiday outside East Anglia at the time so the idea of a transatlantic flight and a tour around the UK staying in hotels sounded both grand and very expensive. Mostly the American visitors were on organised tours which included many places my parents had not been to then, like Edinburgh, York and Oxford and the visitors broke their tour for a day when their group arrived at Cambridge, sixteen miles away, hired a car and made the diversion to the Fens. Very occasionally tours made it to Ely itself but mostly it was a day at the Cambridge colleges that they sacrificed for the purpose of researching their family history. No one I knew had been abroad then other than the men who had been in the army during the second world war, in India and Burma like my father who had been a prisoner-of-war working on the Burma railway leaving many local men frail and 'suffering with their nerves' for the rest of their lives which was how Post-Traumatic Stress Disorder was described then.

All the arrangements for the American visitors had to be made by airmail letters before the Americans left home as my parents did not have a telephone until 1973 when I went away to teacher training college in London.

Childhood

Throughout my childhood if we needed a phone, and we seldom did because no one we knew had a phone, we used a red public telephone box about 100 metres away from the house opposite the local pub called The Rifleman's Arms where our neighbour, a widow called Mina Twite, collected her daily ration of a bottle of Guinness, the Irish milk stout beer, which was issued on prescription from her GP. (From the 1920s, Guinness was believed at the time to be rich in iron and was advertised under the slogan, 'Guinness is good for you', based on anecdotal reports from drinkers who said they felt better after a bottle of Guinness. The brewery wrote to doctors to solicit their views.)

In those days pubs had a bar and lounge, but also an off-licence to which there was a separate entrance. You went into a tiny space which was at the far end of the bar so the landlady, never a landlord, could come to the end of the bar to a little hatch with opaque coloured glass and serve you. You could see into the bar area but you didn't need to walk through it. I knew this space well because from an early age I was sent there to buy cigarettes for my parents, which I hated both because the window was so high and because there was a sign saying that anyone under eighteen would not be served. Across the road from our house was the Ely Beet Sugar sports and social club where there was a hall, bowling greens and tennis courts for the workers and somehow my parents could attend, and which we all did from time to time. I had no qualms about our weekly visit to the 'Sugar Beet', or more properly Ely Beet Sugar Social Club, which was opposite our house and where we all played Bingo for money and drank shandy. Only as an adult did it strike me that this was not an appropriate place for an eight-year old to be when asked where I was when President Kennedy died (November 22 1963). For some reason, probably as a degree of gentrification hit Ely, the pub was later renamed The Tinker of

Ely but its new name did not save it from the bulldozer and it was demolished to make way for a new housing development as Ely began to become popular as a commuter town for Cambridge.

Our house was on the main A10 road that ran from London to King's Lynn, the Lynn Road, now bypassed. It was an extremely busy road and, because of it, from my earliest childhood I was aware of what was called the 'campaign'. That was the period every year which started with the sugar beet harvest in September or October and lasted to the end of beet processing in February or March. During this period lorries piled high with beets which resembled ugly large discoloured white parsnips, hammered up and down the A10 past my bedroom window all hours of the day and night shaking the windows and door. The pounding of the lorries on the road was such an insistent rhythmic sensation that when it stopped in the late Spring there would be weeks when I couldn't sleep and lay awake as if waiting for it to resume.

British Sugar had a factory, built in 1925, at Queen Adelaide, and during the 'campaign' it worked day and night with the lorries travelling from farms across the county and beyond. The lorries passing our house were going back and forth between Cambridgeshire and Norfolk. Within miles of the factory you would experience a dense atmosphere with a pungent smell from the factory like that of a heavy dank pond with a caramel edge. Today, most people do not realise the importance of the sugar beet to the East of England economy but in Ely there were farmers, factory workers and lorry drivers and their families all dependent on it. Queen Adelaide, a hamlet named after a pub, named after Queen Adelaide of Saxe-Meiningen (wife of William IV: she died in 1849), was a strange place with only a few houses but it had three railway crossings in close proximity. In the 1960s all the gates were opened and shut manually so, as sometimes happened, cars would be stopped three times and at each crossing would need to wait as a man would climb down from his box by the track to close the gates, return to his box until the train had passed and then come down again to open them. There was never any sense of urgency and sometimes he would stop and pass the time of day with a motorist if he knew them. In the late winter afternoons a single car might be waiting at one closed railway gate with another closed gate less than 100 yards behind creating a sense of being trapped between gates and exposed only to the low fog and acrid smell from the beet factory.

The Mina Twite who drank Guiness had the end of terrace house next to ours. She took in lorry drivers as lodgers to augment her pension including during 'the campaign'. She had lived in the house since before the second world war. Her late husband had been a lorry driver. She was fascinating to me as a young child. I hardly ever went into her house but very occasionally she would invite me in if she had made some jam tarts. I remember the rooms being very dark with brown and cream painted walls. There was a fly paper hanging down from a glass globe in the middle of the ceiling in the kitchen and sitting room, and dead insects, attracted by the sugary substance on the paper, would accumulate throughout the day. She seemed like a very old lady to me although in 1960 when I first became aware of her she was actually only 61. She always wore a full-length apron, or pinny, over her clothes, which crossed over at the front and was tied at the back. Her slippers were tartan with buttoned down flaps and a beige pompon on each toe. She always wore a hairnet. I don't remember ever seeing her in anything other than her pinny and slippers. At that time long-distance lorry drivers had access to lists of reliable landladies and Mrs Twite seemed to attract a steady stream of lodgers, mostly for a night or two at most but sometimes for longer stays. In the mid-1960s she often had two young men who were brothers, Peter and Brian. She was particularly busy during the sugar beet campaign. Her accommodation must have been very basic, as she did not have a bathroom and the lavatory was outside the house. and I think she took up hot water in a pitcher in the morning so the lodgers could wash using a bowl on a wooden table. There was a good deal of neighbourly chit-chat between my mother and Mrs Twite in the garden or across a fence that divided the area between our back doors which I would overhear. She would often be complaining about the lodgers' habits with chamber pots. Some would use them on the bedspread, rather than on the floor, staining the linen and necessitating extra laundry. In winter others would put the chamber pot under the bed after using them and the warm vapours would rust the underside of the bed springs. All the lodgers were heavy drinkers who stayed out late particularly on Friday and Saturday nights. The walls between our houses were very thin and I could often hear neighbours on both sides vomiting after a heavy night's drinking. I remember the two brothers, Peter and Brian Wright, who stayed often, sometimes together, other times separately. Peter the younger one, aged thirty, took his own life one Saturday night. On the Sunday morning – I was about nine – I was aware that something was amiss with Mrs Twite next door. Mrs Twite's latest lodger hadn't stirred by late morning and she called in my mother who came back and told my father to take me to visit my aunt and uncle in Soham. We returned too soon and outside our house there was a large black hearse: the lodger had been found dead. He was one of the brothers that were regulars. He was thirty years old. As my bedroom backed onto his I felt his presence for years after. That was the end of Mrs Twite's lodgers.

The Americans

Later American visitors to our house would come armed with certificates from Ellis Island, which had been used to process

INA CLEMENTS (THIRD FROM RIGHT) WITH MY FAMILY, 1960

immigrant to the USA from 1892 to 1954, and photographs and home-produced booklets full of stories of the emigrants' experiences as homesteaders. But Ina Clements was working from what she knew from her father, Samuel Clements Junior, and her great-aunt Sarah and great-uncle John who lived into old age and were also Rhoda and John Clements' children, whom Ina had known well and who had followed Samuel Clements as emigrants to America with his wife Mary, and would have remembered the Fenland they left behind.

These American relatives who visited us in the 1960s were considerably more prosperous than we were and usually they came to collect my father in a hired car – Ina Clements had a driver too – and my father would guide them round Ely and the Fen villages including Prickwillow three miles east of Ely, the village that Samuel Clements Junior had left as a two-year-old boy, and Littleport, five miles to the north where Rhoda Francis

Clements had been baptised, taking in the rivers Lark, the Great Ouse and the Little Ouse, and the expansive farmland and tiny villages between. It would have been impossible then as now to get around the Fens without private transport. They would certainly have driven along the River Lark and although my father never mentioned to me that his family had lived along those riverbanks, he must have shown the visitors the farms his relatives had worked on because when the party returned to our house in Ely the American cousins would be full of stories of what they had seen. They had usually visited Ely Cathedral because many of the ancestors had been baptised or married in the Lady Chapel which was the parish church for Ely Trinity between 1566 and 1938, taking in the villages between Ely towards Mildenhall in Suffolk. In my childhood there was still a parish room for Holy Trinity in Ely at the corner of Newnham Street and Nutholt Lane built in the late 1890s, and we often wondered about its name as the two Anglian churches in Ely were called St Mary and St Peter. In fact a parish church was attached to Ely Cathedral at one point and then its duties transferred to the Lady Chapel.

The Americans would have visited Prickwillow and my father would have told them about the fen drainage projects and the re-routing of the River Ouse in 1829-30, something Rhoda and John Clements must have witnessed, and how the area suffered from subsidence because unlike Ely and older villages like Littleport or Stuntney, Prickwillow is part of the Fen itself, not a settlement built on higher dry land. Prickwillow vicarage would have been on the list of places to visit, as it is a spectacular example of peat shrinkage – a consequence of the drainage projects – as the original two steps to its front door when built in the late 1870s had been augmented by a further nine by this time. There were no gravestones with the Clements name to visit as the families were too poor for that, and in any case there was no graveyard in Prickwillow because the fenland with its high water table could not sustain one. Nor would there have been parish records in Prickwillow for the period when Samuel Clements lived there as the village did not become a parish in its own right until the 1870s although a temporary church and school was put up shortly after he left which Rhoda and the family might have used but it too became unsafe because of the sinking peat soil. Sometimes a visit to St Peter's Church in Prickwillow to see its impressive marble font would have resulted in an encounter with a villager who filled in some local detail which would be much appreciated by the Americans. The church closed down in 2011 and it now a private dwelling, as is the primary school which was erected in 1862 and accommodated 220 children.

My father's older sisters, Flo and Rose (whose name was really Rhoda like her great-grandmother) from Littleport and Soham would have arrived at our house by the time my father and the party returned, and perhaps their cousin, Tot (another Rhoda), and her husband George Peacock, and we would all have a sit-down tea which always involved salmon sandwiches (tinned salmon with vinegar was a luxury for Sundays only), ham sandwiches, scones, cake and lots of tea. After tea the Americans would quiz my aunts about their parents and grandparents, and about life in the Fens: information on our side was scant but my widowed Aunt Flo who had been born in 1903, had worked on the land all her life and spoke with a broad Fen accent which fascinated them. She gave them local words like 'dockey' or 'dockey bag' for packed lunches during farm work apparently so-called because pay was 'docked' for the time spent eating; 'ague' was the fen 'malaria' that was quite famous and a reason some people fled the Fens, and another phrase was 'Fen Blows' which happened when the light black soil blew across the roads like a snow-storm during heavy winds – this was a feature of my childhood. To children Aunt Flo would say, 'Thass a davill' and of me to my mother, 'She's a rite little davill, Anne'. My father spoke with a less broad Fen accent, more in pronunciation than using local words or phrases although he would use phrases like 'lazy ol' wind' meaning it cuts right through you, answer 'fair to middlin'' when asked how he was and the days of the week were 'Sun-dee' and 'Mon-dee'. My mother always thought that Aunt Rose, seven years older than my father, was a cut above the rest of the family because she had married out of agricultural work, to a carpenter, and lost her Fen accent completely.

After an exchange of information and because the American visitors always came in the summer, and photographs were never taken indoors or in the winter then, my father would take photographs of us all in our back garden with me in the front of the adults wearing a party dress and a ribbon in my hair and the photograph was sent on to America by post the following Christmas. My father was an enthusiastic photographer, subscribing to 'Amateur Photographer', but he would never have rushed to use up a film so sometimes weeks or months would elapse between a specific photograph and sending the film off in a pre-paid envelope to be processed. Our photographs were almost certainly kept and passed around in America because our history seemed to be as familiar to subsequent visitors as it was to us. My father drew a family tree on the back of an old roll of left-over wallpaper and with every visitor the tree grew with more names year on year. Later visitors had other local stops to make to other relatives that had come to light through their research, some of whom were related and vaguely known to us, others not known even though they only lived a few miles away, and others still who were in-laws of the Americans and not related to us at all. Our American cousins had fared well in the United States and were civil servants, teachers, doctors and farmers: my mother felt the difference in our financial situations keenly, always embarrassed that our house was rented, we didn't at that time even have a toilet indoors and we only had the most basic of bathrooms with a bath but no washbasin. Doubtless the Americans found our circumstances quaint and indicative of how far their families had come since they left the Fens in the 1850s.

CHAPTER 6

Rhoda Francis Clements

Burnt Fen 1801

The ancestor whom we and these American visitors shared, Rhoda Francis, was great-grandmother to both Ina Clements and to my father, his sisters and their cousin. She was born in 1801 in Littleport in Cambridgeshire, not in the village itself as her father, William Francis, was an agricultural labourer and they lived in a labourers' cottages located near the farms that had been recovered through drainage, in Burnt Fen. Rhoda Francis was the youngest of ten children in the Francis family. As a child my father would explain to me how the Cambridgeshire Fens had been mostly under water until the Dutch engineer, Cornelius Vermuyden, had been brought to the Fens from the Netherlands by the King to oversee the drainage of the area in the mid-seventeenth century by cutting two artificial waterways twenty miles apart to create a floodplain that provided wetlands for the wildfowl we went to see every winter at Welney Wash, between Ely and Wisbech, so allowing the rivers to flood in a managed way. The drainage projects exposed the rich farmlands that my male ancestors, and some female ones too, spent long hours working as agricultural labourers but the exposed peat brought other problems as it shrank year on year. My ancestors would have witnessed the change from windmills to steam pumping engines which pumped the water from the land up from the drains and dykes into the outflow channels and up into the rivers. Our American visitors assumed that their relatives had had a role in the drainage schemes but this is unlikely as the seventeenth-century schemes were managed by proto-venture capitalists who brought in labour from outside the area, including at least five hundred Scottish prisoners following the Battle of Dunbar (1650), and Dutch prisoners too. The 'adventurers' as they were called invested in the drainage schemes in return for gaining the promised rich farming land.

Drainage was, until the seventeenth century, a piecemeal operation with different landowners draining, sometimes successfully, areas of land but until Francis Russell, the Fourth Earl of Bedford (1587-1641), who had family land in the Thorney area, took an interest there had been no area-wide proposals. Until then the area was grassy in the summers when cattle could graze, but water-logged in the winters. The local people were considered wild and uncivil. I have already discussed the 17th century changes to the Fens, but will add that a 1600 Act of Parliament permitted landowners to exchange drained land to those willing to drain them. The Crown owned a number of estates, and James I encouraged the Ely sewage commissioners to seek out individuals prepared to take on drainage projects. Early attempts worked to some degree although there were disputes about what constituted successful drainage. Local 'Fen Tigers', named after the original resistant Fenlanders, with 'tiger', according to James Boyce, probably coming from the Welsh 'tioga' meaning 'peasant' rather than the big cat, would have fought the developers by sabotaging the drainage efforts in the seventeenth century as they saw their traditional way of life, eel-catching, fishing, wild-fowling and reed-cutting, threatened and so were more likely to have opposed the works than contributed to them. Only with the steam pumps of the early nineteenth century was the battle between the developers and the local people fully won.

Littleport May 1816

Rhoda Francis, youngest of ten children, was baptised in St George's Church, Littleport in September 1801. The baptism service was almost certainly taken by the Reverend John Vachell as he had been the local vicar since 1795, had married in 1796 and five of his children were born and baptised in Littleport including a daughter Mary Ann Vachell who was baptised exactly two months after Rhoda Francis. John Vachell's memorial plaque is on the side of the church of St Peter and St Paul in Aldeburgh, Suffolk. A son, George Harvey Vachell, was born in Littleport during his father's time as vicar, educated at Harrow, and became chaplain for the East India Company, living in Macao and Canton in China in the 1820s and 1830s, where he conducted baptisms, weddings and burials. Many of the gravestones of those he buried are in the Protestant Cemetery in Macao which we have visited several times. Lindsay and May Ride's book about Macao suggests that Vachell Junior had a reputation for fine living, gambling and flirting but he was seemingly a devoted son to the extent of funding a handsome burial stone 'erected…as a token of filial affection' in 1830 in Aldeburgh where his father died. Reverend John Vachell, was well-known in the Ely and Littleport area both as the vicar and as an unpopular, because strict, magistrate, and he would feature in the story of Littleport.

On July 15 1814 there was a celebration of the signing of the Treaties of Paris in Ely following the Napoleonic wars. There had been fireworks, parades and a special dinner with military bands and a procession through the town. Two years later spirits were lower with many agricultural workers were experiencing poverty.

Fifteen years after her baptism, Rhoda Francis would have witnessed the extraordinary events of the summer of 1816 when for a period of two months in May and June Littleport and Ely were the focus for a period of extreme social unrest. I knew about the Littleport Riots because there was a plaque on the side of the wall of St Mary's Church Ely which commemorated the five men who were hanged on 28 June 1816 with the warning, 'May their awful fate be a warning to others', but I never thought much about the executions or where they would have happened, or indeed who else had been involved. At St Mary's Junior School in Silver Street, Ely in the 1960s, every Thursday during my final year we were marched round the corner, past the almshouses where my mother would live in the late 1990s, and Oliver Cromwell's house, to St Mary's church for a service instead of a school assembly. On one occasion we must have been shown the plaque. The five condemned men were taken from Ely Gaol in an open cart, and with some ceremony driven to a site in St John's Road where they were publicly hanged at 11 am on the morning of Friday, June 28th 1816. The vicar of St Mary's Church allowed them to be buried together in one grave in the church grounds near where the plaque is now. It is clear from the records that the event attracted a great crowd, and I wonder whether people came in from the surrounding villages much as they would for market days, or events like Hospital Sunday which was a popular event in the 1960s and 1970s, involving 'floats' on lorries that we decorated and paraded around the streets of Ely in a procession to raise money for the Ely hospital(s) (the Tower Hospital where my father worked as a porter towards the end of his working life located in the former Ely Workhouse and the RAF Hospital on the A10 road towards Littleport). Throughout my primary school years a group of us would spend every Thursday market day of the school holidays at the weekly 'pig market' which took place behind Newnham

Street. There were very few restrictions on children in the early 1960s and even from the age of seven or eight we would take off for the day in the morning and not be expected back until teatime. On Market Days the Ely streets were busy, there were stalls on the market square, and buses coming and going from the villages to the bus stops all along Market Street. Sometimes we would include a visit to the cathedral which was free to visit in those days and play on the maze under the West Tower, an innovation added when Gilbert Scott restored Ely Cathedral in the second half of the nineteenth century, the first, longest and most successful of his cathedral renovations and a project which Rhoda Clements must have been aware of. Or we would climb the tower and take in the vast expanse of fen countryside to be seen from there.

With a population of only 1850 people living in the Littleport area in 1816, it is inconceivable that Rhoda Francis and her family would not have known some of those involved in the riots: the two hundred rioters themselves, the families in Littleport whose houses were damaged and robbed, or the farmers and magistrates who tried to contain them which included the Rev John Vachell who had baptised many of them at St George's in Littleport. The Littleport Riots took place over forty-eight hours in May 1816 following a meeting of about fifty members of the Littleport Benefits Club at the Globe Inn in Main Street Littleport. The trial reports cite 'threats and excesses in another part of the country, under the pretence of the lowness of wages and high price of provision' and it seems that demonstrations in nearby Southery may have inspired the Littleport men to demand increases in pay. On the evening of Wednesday 22 May 1816, some two hundred local people took to the streets in Littleport with pitchforks and bludgeons and went from house to house demanding money and breaking up houses. One target was Henry Martin, one of a few significant landowners who had benefited from Parliamentary

JOHN VACHELL'S PLAQUE AT ALDEBURGH CHURCH IN SUFFOLK

Enclosure, and who was very unpopular with the farm workers. Another was the Rev. Vachell at the vicarage in Church Lane. The men arrived at the vicarage, then opposite the Littleport parish church, demanding money. Initially tempted to try appeasement Vachell gave over some money and offered to discuss the men's demands but when they asked for more, he went off and returned with a pistol which angered the crowd. They piled into the house. Vachell, his wife and daughters escaped – the sons were away at boarding school – making their way to Ely while the crowd caused significant damage to the property and took silver spoons and other items. After the trial Vachell successfully sued the Ely

Hundred for damages under the Riot Act and was awarded £708 (around £60,000 in today's money), making him even more unpopular than he already was with the local people. My parents would have considered that a typical example of the privileged feathering their nests leaving the poor to fend for themselves. The cost of the settlement had to be raised in levies and probably contributed to Vachell recognising that he needed to leave the area for good. He negotiated an arrangement whereby he stayed on as Littleport vicar in name only while a succession of curates took his place while he retired to Aldeburgh in Suffolk, and died 1830 'after many years of severe infirmity' presumably dating back to his experience in the Riots.

The rioters moved from Littleport to Ely with a wagon and four horses and armed with pitchforks, cleavers and at least one punt gun, arriving in Ely in the early hours of the morning, presumably not far from where the Royal Air Force Hospital would be built in 1939 for second world war casualties. (My mother worked at the RAF base for many years as a batwoman to the RAF nursing sisters. The hospital provided local healthcare services from the time of the National Health Service in 1948, my father died there in 1986 and my cousin's twins were born there in the late 1980s when the hospital was still run by the Military and the babies were taken away and brought to their mothers strictly every four hours.) There had been a toll-gate on what became the A10 on the way out of Ely towards Littleport which cannot have been far away from the hospital. The Ely magistrates had been forewarned by one Littleport man who had fled to Ely when the unrest started and one magistrate met the rioters at the toll-gate and persuaded them to congregate in the Market Square in Ely. There was no love lost between labouring men and the clergy who as educated men allied themselves with the magistrates and farmers, and often were magistrates themselves. The rioters said that their children were starving and they demanded the price of a stone of flour per day. The Magistrates were initially minded to placate the men and agreed that they would pay each poor family two shillings per head per week when a stone of flour cost half-a-crown, the allowance to be amended if the price of flour increased or decreased. They instructed local farmers that the price of labour should be two shillings per day, and that labourers should be paid in full by the farmer that hired him. Presumably this was not always the case. The men demanded 'forgiveness for what had passed' which seems to have been a sticking point and agreed as first as long as they returned to their own homes immediately. About three quarters of the crowd left but others stayed on and continued looting. Eventually the remaining rioters returned to Littleport and congregated inside the George and Dragon Inn in Station Road. One of the clergymen-magistrates wrote to the Home Secretary, Viscount Sidmouth (Henry Addington, 1757-1844), for advice about a pardon which seems to have escalated the incident and opened the way for using it as a means of deterring other potential insurrectionists across the country. Sidmouth seems to have had a personal mission to counter any hint of revolutionary movements. On Thursday, 23 May the Royal Dragoons arrived in Ely from Bury St Edmunds and the next day they went on to Littleport where they managed to get the rioters out of the pub and line them up outside. There was a bit of a kerfuffle resulting in one man being shot dead and another wounded. This subdued the mob and the soldiers were able to arrest about seventy people who were all taken to Ely Gaol.

Ely June 1816

The trial took place before three judges, two from London and a local judge, from 17-22 June 1816 and must have attracted large crowds. Contemporary reports record that before the hearing, as was normal before the local assizes in the Isle of Ely, started with a number of 'respectable' people gathering to meet the judges, there was a breakfast at the Bishop's Palace for the judges followed by a service at Ely Cathedral which set the tone for the proceedings, the aim of which was to deter further uprisings. From the very outset the view seems to have been that the instigators of the riots were not poor enough to have a genuine grievance in a country that did more than any other to provide for the poor. The hearings took place over six days. Some cases were dropped. Twenty-three men and one woman were found guilty of 'divers robberies during the riots at Ely and Littleport'. Nine men and one woman were sentenced to 12 months in prison. Nine were transported to New South Wales. Five men were condemned to death. A contemporary commentary of the trial lays out the circumstances in England at the time, 'the stagnation in our manufactories in consequence

PLAQUE FROM ST MARY'S CHURCH, ELY

Memoir of the Fens: An Ely Education

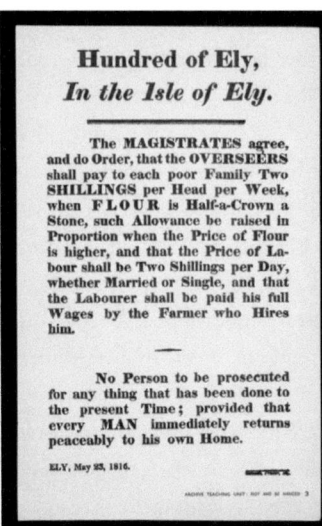

THE MAGISTRATES' OFFER TO THE LITTLEPORT RIOTERS, 1816

of the depressed state of commerce', 'the number of men …thrown upon the country without the means of employment…of subsistence', 'farmers forced to emigrate because they could not meet rents and taxes', but in Ely 'a settled plan of disorder, of rapine, and violence, seems to have been formed, and carried into execution, partly too by men who were in none of the situations we have described…' and there was a view of the inhabitants of the Fens as 'more rude and uncivilised than in any other district'. There is little record of how the Littleport riots and their consequences affected the people of the area although I suspect that the events consolidated a mistrust of the authorities, both church and secular as even in the 1960s there was a sense in my wider family that there was no support for working people to be found from anyone in any sort of formal role whether magistrate, local councillor, clergy and certainly not the MP. Sir Harry Legge-Bourke MP was everything my parents despised: educated at Eton and Sandhurst, Conservative and installed it seemed for life, having been elected to the Isle of Ely constituency in 1945, and lasting till his death in 1973 (his granddaughter, 'Tiggy' Legge-Bourke, nanny to William and Harry, shows how privilege replicates itself).

Prickwillow 1820

Three years after the summer of 1816 my great great-grandmother Rhoda Francis met a farm labourer from Mildenhall in Suffolk called John Clements. I know very little about him as it is hard to locate him in parish records before he married Rhoda. They were married in November 1819 in Holy Trinity Church, the Lady Chapel, in Ely. I do not know for certain exactly where Rhoda and John Clements lived in the first years of their marriage because their children's birthplaces were variously given as Prickwillow, Ely, or Burnt Fen which is towards Mildenhall and Littleport, and sometimes a child is given different birth places across different censuses, so it is possible that the family moved around the area between those places as agricultural work and accommodation became available but it is equally possible that the places where they lived were remote and differently described over the years. By the 1840s John and Rhoda Clements were established in a labourer's cottage in Branch Bank which is a road along the River Lark near Prickwillow. The River Lark is a tributary of the Great Ouse – it would have been easy to get from Prickwillow to Isleham and Soham, or to Littleport by boat, or into Suffolk along the river through Mildenhall to Bury St Edmunds. You can walk along the Lark today: the landscape is the same as when the droves across the farmland were first created to make paths through the Fen and there is little evidence of any modernisation. The area still feels remote with large expanses of agricultural land, immense skies and a very few houses dotted along the edges of the farms so as not to steal valuable land, including Tom's Farm which is listed in the nineteenth century censuses and still there today. The river-banks are high above the road on both sides and today you can walk along the top of them with the river at roughly the same level as the path but the road some nine or ten feet below.

Rhoda and John Clements' first child, Mary Clements was

THE CONFLUENCE OF THE RIVER OUSE AND THE RIVER LARK TODAY

born in 1820 and baptised in the Lady Chapel in Ely. By 1841 when John was forty-three and Rhoda forty, they had had nine children of which only one, another Rhoda born in 1824, had died in childhood, and the five who were still under fourteen lived with them at home. The older children, Mary, James and Samuel had left home at thirteen for jobs as live-in general servants or farm labourers. Mary and James Clements were employed as servants in Little Downham with different branches of the Moxon family who were local farmers. Little Downham was another village dating from the time of the Domesday Book six miles away on the other side of Ely. In Branch Bank the Clements family had a lodger, William King, an agricultural labourer, possibly the same William King who would marry their eldest daughter Mary Clements.

In May 1847 Rhoda and John Clements' son Samuel (1826-1863), who was then twenty-one years old, married a widow, Mary

Bottom, from Soham. Samuel Clements may have been working as a labourer in the Soham Fen travelling by water along the River Lark. His new wife was thirty, the widow of Jeremiah Bottom, another agricultural labourer. Samuel Clements may have worked with Jeremiah Bottom and known the family, or he may have got to know Mary Bottom after her husband's death. It would not have been easy for Mary Rhodes Bottom with no husband and five young sons on her own, the youngest, Jerry, born just eight months before his father's death. On marriage Samuel Clements brought his new wife Mary and her five boys all under twelve to live in a labourer's cottage in Padnal Fen across the River Lark from his parents on Branch Bank, and shortly after the marriage a daughter was born. When a further child came along in 1852 Samuel and Mary Clements must have started to consider ways of improving their lot and with this in mind Samuel Clements set out for New York from Liverpool in April 1854, leaving his wife behind with the seven children. Two months after Samuel Clements' arrival in New York Mary Clements gave birth to her eighth child, Samuel Junior, Ina Clements' father. We do not know what Rhoda Clements thought of her son's departure for Liverpool and on to New York leaving behind a wife with eight children. Mary Clements and her family remained in the labourer's cottage and the calculation must have been that the four older Bottom boys, Samuel Clements' step-sons, by now in their mid to late teens would be capable of earning enough as labourers to keep Mary and her family until it was clear what prospects there were for them all in America. Rhoda Clements would never see her son again and in 1854 Samuel Clements wrote to his wife and family with instructions to leave the Fens to join him in Illinois, hence Mary, Samuel's five step-sons and their three children left the Fens. Accompanying them was Rhoda's twenty-three-year old son John Clements and his sister, eighteen year-old Sarah Clements who left

THE VIEW FROM BRANCH BANK TODAY WITH ELY CATHEDRAL IN THE DISTANCE

with Mary and the children for the United States never to return. Sarah Clements would later marry her step-nephew, John Bottom who was twenty when they emigrated and maybe the prospect of marriage to John Bottom was the reason she was determined to emigrate with her sister-in-law.

Missing from the 1851 census is John and Rhoda Clements' second child, James Clements, now thirty, who either died or left the country sometime after 1843 when he was a witness at his sister Mary Clements' wedding to William King. There is no trace of him in England after that time, nor a record of his death. An Australian family has claimed him online with a story that he was convicted of a minor crime, perhaps poaching, at the Cambridge Assizes and given a sentence of seven years transportation to Australia where he stayed, and there is some evidence that he settled and died in Gawler River near Adelaide in 1882. Rhoda Clements certainly never saw him after 1844 and I wonder how common it was for local men to be transported to Australia for seven or fourteen years or indeed for life. Few seemed to have returned and Rhoda would have been aware of the nine Littleport rioters transported in 1816.

Widowed

Rhoda Francis Clements was forty-eight when her youngest child, Richard, was born in 1849. Things were beginning to change in the area which had been dominated by agricultural work. By 1851 railway cottages were emerging nearby near what is currently Shippea Hill where a small number of labourers were living. Over the next few years increasing numbers of railway workers would move into the area but I suspect Rhoda Clements never used a train. She was widowed in 1861. By then three children were in the United States and Samuel would die there two years later. One son was probably in Australia. Two girls, both named Rhoda, had died in childhood. A daughter, Maria Clements, left Prickwillow for South London at the age of seventeen in the early 1850s and never returned. Only Robert, Job and my great-grandfather William were still living and working as agricultural labourers in the Fens when Rhoda died.

Soham 1866

In 1866 Rhoda re-married – to James Haylock Boatright, a widower born in Dullingham just south of Newmarket (and somewhere I camped as a Girl Guide in the 1970s), who had settled in Soham not far from where Mary Bottom, Rhoda Clements' daughter-in-law had lived. He and Rhoda lived together in a house in the Soham Fen for nine years. When he died in 1875 she moved in with her son Robert. By accident or design she allowed or encouraged her children to branch out and leave the Fens where there was no future for them. Mostly they did well but she never saw those that left again. The only photographs I have of Rhoda Clements' children are of Samuel Clements, already looking like an American in a checked waistcoat and cravat taken in Illinois in the early 1860s, and the photograph that Ina Clements, our first American visitor, took of Samuel's sister and brother, Sarah and John Clements, taken when they were in old age. There are no graves for John Clements, Rhoda or James Boatwright. They live on online only.

CHAPTER 7

The Clements

Rachel, Hannah and Sarah Clements were the daughters of William Clements and his wife Mary. Rachel, my grandmother, was the youngest of nine children, three boys and six girls. William Clements was one of the four of Rhoda and John Clements' twelve children who stayed in the Fens; and the three boys, Robert, Job and William were all farm labourers from the age of thirteen.

Mary Seaber, the mother, came from further along the River Lark from Prickwillow where the Clements family lived, towards Suffolk, from an old Cambridgeshire village called Isleham which would have been easily accessible by river from Prickwillow when they met and then married in 1860. Isleham has a priory building dating back to the eleventh century now run by English Heritage, originally part of a French religious house. The village of Isleham, thinly disguised as Gislea – the name Isleham originates from Gisla-ham – would briefly become famous in 1975 when Mary Chamberlain published *Fenwomen,* a book drawn from an oral history project interviewing local women about their lives living in a Fenland village, and the first title to come out with Virago Press, the feminist publishing house founded by Carmen Calill in the 1970s. Mary Chamberlain said she wanted to produce a book

SAMUEL CLEMENTS IN THE
EARLY 1860S

like *Akenfield*, the 'portrait of a village' by the Suffolk writer Ronald Blythe written in 1969 and made into a film by Peter Hall in 1974, but acknowledging the lives of women living in the small remote fenland village. The *Cambridge Evening News*, the local evening paper, ran a week of stories at the time implying that *Fenwomen* included lurid confessions by the women featured in the book but it was a record of very matter-of-fact interviews with Isleham women about their lives and memories, and about the isolation of the village of Isleham, a sense that still resonated with anyone growing up in the Fens in the 1960s and 1970s. Caryl Churchill adapted the book into a play, *Fen*, which we saw at the University of Essex theatre when we lived in Colchester in the early 1980s in a production that opened with women stretched across the stage in rows bending over the flat fields, a scene I recognised because in the summer of 1968 my mother and her friend had a job onion wringing in some similar looking fields and my friend Rosemary and I, both of us thirteen years old, went along as workers – probably illegally – during one school holiday. It was hot work moving slowly up and down the field bending over to gather up the onions which a harvester had left lying in the fields. Our job was to 'wring off' the long bluish-green leaves, leave them in the field, and pack the onions into baskets.

There was very little shelter from the sun because like all fenland fields there were no trees or shady places for workers to rest. Ely Cathedral loomed over us on one side with the flat black fields stretching into the distance on the other. It was piece-work, each worker paid by the number of baskets they had filled at the end of each day, and my friend and I earned enough each to buy white sweaters with red and blue trim crew necks, which were all the rage because of the 'I'm backing Britain' campaign. My parents disapproved of 'I'm backing Britain' which had started when a group of Surbiton secretaries volunteered an extra half hour a day of unpaid work to gee up the then-flagging UK economy. The Government leapt on the scheme, getting the endorsement of the Duke of Edinburgh, but my parents saw it as exploitative of working people by getting them to subsidise employers with free labour. There are photographs of us wearing the sweaters with flared trousers, bells round our necks and carrying paper union jack carrier bags – it was the year after 'the summer of love' and we wanted to be hippies.

By the time my grandmother, Rachel Clements, was born in 1877 William and Mary Clements (née Seaber) had been married for seventeen years and already had three sons and five daughters with the oldest, John Clements, aged fifteen, already working as a farm labourer. Soon after the birth of Rachel the family moved from Burnt Fen where William Clements, now in his mid-forties, was a farm servant, to St John's Place on the edges of Ely, one of the oldest settlement areas where today you can see the remains of a medieval hospital and barn, and where William was able to combine the role of milkman with farm labouring so this probably represented a step-up in the family's income.

By 1881 one daughter had died at the age of eleven in the Dead Mill (Roswell) Pits on the eastern edge of Ely. The 'pits' arose from 'gaulting', digging up clay to reinforce the river banks, and they are about eight hectares in size. As a child I remember a hunt for a local missing boy concluded with the news that he had drowned in the pits. Mary Ann Clements, my grandmother's sister, died in similar circumstances. Another, Hannah Clements, was in service, and a son, Frederick, who, at the age of seventeen, had decided to leave the Fens and move up to Eston, on the edges of Middlesbrough, and lodge with an uncle who had left the Fens for the Eston Iron Ore mines some years before. Following the discovery of iron ore in Eston in the 1840s, many agricultural labourers moved into Eston and Teeside from the countryside to find work in the mines, expanding the local population from around 600 people in the 1840s to over 90,000 by the end of the century. After a period of living with his uncle and aunt, Frederick Clements married a young woman from Beamish, a village in County Durham, and settled in the North-East for the rest of his life and they had eleven children. Frederick Clements was three years older than his sister Rhoda and the two were probably close – Frederick named his first child Rhoda – and it seems that Frederick was keen to have his sister nearby and suggested her for a role – or 'spoke for her' as was said – as general servant to a retired master mariner, John Clernit Murray, and his older widowed sister who were living in Chirton, North Shields. Rhoda Clements was probably under some pressure from her parents to find work from the age of thirteen and may have already had a prior role as a servant in the Cambridgeshire area but sometime in the decade 1881-1891 Frederick Clements suggested Rhoda for the position. Frederick had been in North Shields for some time by then, was married with a child, and was working as a signalman for the River Tyne Commissioners where he must have met John Clernit Murray who made it known that he and his sister were looking for a servant girl and so, at Frederick Clements' suggestion, Rhoda Clements travelled up from Cambridgeshire to become their sole servant. Sometime after Rhoda Clements was established in the house John Clernit Murray's sister moved on and in 1897 Rhoda Clements married John Clernit Murray, by then in his early sixties and retired. Rhoda Clements was thirty-one when she married. It seems unlikely that she ever returned home to Cambridgeshire or saw her sisters or parents again, and there is little information about her married life other than that there were no children and that on her death she left £425, equivalent to several thousand pounds at today's prices, to her husband. In 1908 at the age of forty-two she was admitted to the Morpeth Asylum as a lunatic and died there a few days later.

When Rhoda Clements Murray died her brother Frederick Clements and John Clernit Murray must have still been in contact because soon after Rhoda's death two of Frederick Clements' own daughters, nieces of Rhoda Clements, moved in with John Clernit Murray as servants. Another Rhoda Clements, John Clernit Murray's late wife's niece, aged 20 became his housekeeper, and her younger sister, Martha Jane Clements, 18, was the maid. It is hard to believe that John Clernit Murray needed two servants so perhaps it was Frederick Clements' suggestion that his two older daughters should take on the task of running the household for him together in place of their aunt, his late wife, and it was good for Frederick to have his two oldest children in employment. Young Rhoda Clements married in 1912 and almost certainly gave up her job at that point leaving Martha Jane Clements as housekeeper until her own marriage in 1915. John Clernit Murray died in 1918. His father had died when he was very young and he was apprenticed to the merchant navy at the age of eighteen in 1855, working his way up the ranks, from 'able seaman' to 'second seaman' then 'only mate' and finally he retired as a Master Mariner but he had never married until he met Rhoda Clements. It is hard to guess what his eleven years of marriage to Rhoda Clements were like and how the arrangement affected them both.

Rachel Clements had been married for nine years and had four children when her sister, Rhoda Clernit Murray, died in 1908, but she could have hardly known her sister Rhoda, or her older brothers, John and Frederick as both moved away from the Fens as soon as they could. She was closer to the older sister Hannah who remained in the Fens, as a general servant in the 1880s working for a veterinarian and his wife, the Porters, who had two grown-up daughters living with them in Denmark House, in what is now Prickwillow Road (then called Common Road), Ely. She would almost certainly have continued to visit the family particularly when they lived in St John's Place which was an easy walk from where she was living. The two daughters of the Porter family, then in their late twenties, were running a small residential school for governesses. A German governess was boarding with them, a nineteen year-old young woman from Bremen, who was helping with the teaching. There were five girl students boarding in the house. In 1881 two of the students were sisters from Haddenham, about seven miles away, but the other three were from London and Kent suggesting the Miss Porters recruited to their school nationally, and the young women moved on to positions as governesses, so the school was successful. Hannah Clements then in her mid-teens and another girl, two years younger, were general servants and together must have managed all the housework, cooking and laundry for the whole establishment which also included an adult son who was a brewer 'employing one man'. Hannah Clements left the household when, at the age of twenty, she married Thomas Cross, an agricultural worker, in 1885, and moved with her husband to Brank Bank on the River Lark, where, a year later, her father William Clements, newly widowed would move next door, with his daughter helping him with housework.

Hope Brothers Shirt and Collar Factory

Unlike her older sisters for whom the only employment choices at the age of thirteen were land work or living in as a domestic servant, my grandmother, Rachel Clements, managed to avoid both and instead, in the early 1890s, at the age of thirteen, she went to work in the Hope Brothers Shirt and Collar Factory in Littleport. This must have seemed like a very modern thing for a young woman to do in the 1890s, particularly in the Fens where factories were almost unknown. The factory had been set up in 1881 by Thomas Peacock, a successful businessman who had been born in Littleport and trained as a hosier with the store Robert Sayle in Cambridge (later part of the John Lewis Partnership). Thomas Peacock left Robert Sayle to become a merchant working in China and the Far East. When he returned to England, by now wealthy, he set up a gentlemen's tailor retail business in London's Ludgate Hill, but settled his family in one of the few grand houses in Littleport, called The Grange, in the Ely Road. In my childhood the Grange was a convalescent home that had belonged to the Transport and General Workers' Union, and it had been used at the beginning of the second world war as a temporary Royal Air Force hospital ahead of the opening of the new building in Ely in 1940.

By the 1880s Thomas Peacock had a string of shops and decided to cut costs by manufacturing his own shirts and collars, setting up the Hope Brothers factory in his home village of Littleport to provide work for local women and girls. He named it Hope Brothers not because there were any brothers of that name, but to promote 'Hope' in the context of some very poor local harvests in the 1870s. He set up factories in other parts of the country too and had around twenty-four shops and factories at peak. In Littleport Thomas Peacock provided a library, houses and social facilities for the girls and women and he has lately been

HOPE BROTHERS SHIRT AND COLLAR FACTORY, LITTLEPORT

The postcard (left) dated 17th September 1906 to Miss Lizzie Barrett at 14 Palmerston Rd, Wood Greem, from Percy Heffer of Victoria St., Littleport.
Below: The shirt factory.
(Credit: Littleport Society at www.littleportsociety.org.uk)

recognised in Littleport as an important local philanthropist. My grandmother, Rachel Clements, worked in the factory alongside about 400 other women and girls and boarded in Ten Mile Bank which is about five miles from Littleport. In the early 1980s a friend's daughter was in a university placement at the same factory, by then owned by Burberry, and lodging in the same road as an aunt of mine. She did not finish the placement, finding Littleport too isolated and the people too strange. The three-storey Shirt and Collar factory is now flats.

The Dorlings

My grandparents, William Dorling and Rachel Clements married on 14th February 1899 in St Peter's Church in Prickwillow. They moved from Prickwillow where they had started married life to Pond Cottages in Downham Road on the edges of Ely. Around 1912 there are records of their first child, Victoria, attending the Silver Street school: '7 November 1912. Lilly Dorling admitted to Silver Street National School. Left 23 June 1913'. Lilly was eleven when she joined the school and left eighteen months later, on her twelfth birthday. Lilly's guardian was given as Mrs Cross at Pond Cottages, which was Rachel's sister, Hannah, so somehow the tenancy of Pond Cottages must initially have fallen to Hannah and Thomas Cross, and then on to Rachel and her husband William Dorling when Hannah and her family moved to Branch Bank along with the widowed father.

Lilly's sister, Flo, attended the same school from November 1914 when she was eleven, until November 1916, and most likely Annie, Wag, Rose and my father were also there for at least two years each, because once settled in Pond Cottages the Dorlings did not move on. The school that they attended had been built as a pair of National Schools for Boys and Girls in 1859 and was the principal primary school in the town until long after I left Ely.

There had been an infant school in Broad Street built at around the same time but by the time I was at the school – officially called St Mary's and by then a Church of England school on two sites – the Broad Street building had been incorporated within the junior school and augmented with temporary hut-type classrooms. It was where we decamped to from the main Silver Street School site for the duration of what is now year 5. The main building in Silver Street has been demolished now and there are modern houses on the site. The Broad Street building opposite the south gate of Ely Park was a pottery for many years but is now a private residence. My grandmother, Rachel Clements, as the youngest child in her family benefited from the family's time living in Ely because, unlike her sisters and brothers, she also attended the National School in Silver Street Ely from the age of seven in 1884.

William and Rachel Dorling's children, two boys and four girls were all born between 1901 and 1918 and were all pupils at the National Schools in Silver Street but none of them attended school beyond the age of thirteen and none achieved any qualifications. After National School those that could afford to stay on in education would have gone either to Soham Grammar School for Boys, or to the Girls' High School which had been established in 1905 and was then in a building called Bedford House in St Mary's Street, so-named because from 1800 it had been the headquarters of the Bedford Level Corporation which had the responsibility for the drainage and maintenance of the Fens. By all accounts the building was always inadequate for use as a school and by the time I knew it, when it housed Needham's secondary modern school, its grounds were crammed with additional buildings, mostly huts.

My grandparents, Rachel and William Dorling, lived at Pond Cottages in Downham Road for the whole of their married life. The daughters were all married by the mid-1930s, and the

WILLIAM AND RACHEL
DORLING, 1917, WITH (BACK)
FLO, WAG AND LIL AND
(FRONT) RHODA AND ANNIE

sons joined the regular army with the Suffolk Regiment as soon as they could at the age of nineteen. My uncle and father both served in the Second World War and were out of the UK for most of the war years. My father was out of the country from 1937 to 1947. My grandparents took in three evacuees from the Central Foundation Jewish School in London, a young boy and his two older sisters, for the duration of the war when the children came to Ely in 1939 in an arrangement with the Grammar schools.

My grandmother Rachel died in 1949 and my grandfather was taken in by my aunt and died in 1956 the year before my aunt was widowed. Of Rachel's girls two died before their time, Lil in 1950, and the age of 48 and Annie, at the age of 60. Her sons both died in their mid-sixties and two daughters, Flo and Rose lived long lives into their nineties. Rachel's father, William Clements, lived his final years with Rachel's sister, Hannah, in Branch Bank Prickwillow. He died in August 1921, aged 85 years old, 'drowned in the River Ouse'.

CHAPTER 8

Rachel Clements and her family

Ely, 1968

I knew nothing about my paternal grandparents, William and Rachel Dorling, until March 1968, when I was twelve and when my parents had a surprise visit from a relative of my father. It had already been a difficult year for my father's family because his older sister, Annie, had died suddenly in the January. She was sixty years old. In those days before people had telephones her widower, Cyril Gothard, had travelled about ten miles over to Soham from Wilburton where he and Annie lived to tell my Aunt Rose who he knew had a car and so could let the rest of the family know. Aunt Rose drove over to Ely to bring the news to us and then my father went with her to tell their older widowed sister, Flo, who lived in Littleport with her daughter and son-in-law. My father must have written to his older brother in Buxton as he came to Ely a few days later and went with my father and his sisters to the funeral. I am not sure my mother had met Annie or Cyril. She certainly did not know them well and none of the spouses attended the funeral. it was the first I had heard that I had an aunt who lived in Wilburton which was only about six miles away so the whole business of her death was something of a mystery to me. It is clear from photographs taken in the 1920s and 1930s that Annie had been a very attractive young woman and the most delicate of my father's four sisters. Photographs of the other three girls show them working around the farm, laughing, dressing up in my grandfather's army uniform or riding motor bikes but all the pictures of Annie show her in formal clothes with gloves and hat.

Annie was my grandparents', William and Rachel Dorling, fourth child. Her real name was Sarah Ann but she was always known as Annie. (All my father's siblings had official names and names they were known by. The oldest daughter was baptised Victoria May but was always Lil. Floria was Flo, Sarah was Annie, Charles was Wag and Rhoda was Rose. My father was James but was known to everyone as Bill.) Annie had gone into service in her teens and then married Cyril Gothard, an agricultural worker from Wilburton, in 1934 when she was twenty-seven, and from that point on the couple had kept themselves to themselves and had hardly been seen by the wider family other than on odd visits to the parents while they were still alive. Annie gave up paid employment when they married. They had no children. Throughout her marriage Annie suffered with mental health problems, and spent time in the local mental health institution, then just known as 'Fulbourn' by the locals by which they meant the 'lunatic asylum' rather than the rather pleasant leafy village. This was probably why she was not mentioned, as any such issues were only spoken of then very discreetly, 'in hushed tones'. She died at her own hand, having ingested rat poisoning, and after the funeral was not mentioned again. Her widower never remarried and was buried beside her in Wilburton cemetery some twenty years later. My mother had little tolerance of mental illness and her attitude would almost certainly have been that Annie 'had had too much time to think'.

Annie Gothard's death probably prompted her cousin Billy Clements' visit to Cambridgeshire in the Spring of 1968. He would have heard of her death from my uncle as they both lived in Buxton, Derbyshire, and were brothers-in-law as well as cousins, because their mothers were sisters and my uncle had married Billy Clements' step-sister, Sarah Maryain Henderson, known as Mabel, in 1940. Mabel seems to have been a regular visitor to my grandparents, William and Rachel Dorling in Cambridgeshire in the 1930s and there are several photographs of her with my grandmother almost as if they were friends rather than aunt and niece, twenty years apart in age. In December 1923 my uncle joined the Suffolk Regiment which recruited a lot of Ely men at the time, and was away for many of the years leading up to the Second World War. Mabel was a domestic servant and cook for most of the war and lived with three other servant girls in Buxton. He must have been on leave in June 1940s, and Mabel was visiting from Derbyshire, when they married in Ely's St Mary's Church. They were both in their late thirties. When my uncle was de-mobbed in December 1945 they settled at Buxton where they lived together until Mabel died in 1956, almost certainly another suicide. There were no children.

In February 1968 Billy Clements, my uncle's cousin and brother-in-law, appeared on our front doorstep. He was by then a man in his late sixties, dressed all in black and with an 'automatic umbrella'. No one ever knocked at the front door and we certainly had not seen an automatic, self-opening, umbrella before so these were grounds for suspicion from the outset. Our visitor announced that he was William Massie Clements from Buxton in Derbyshire and that he had come to stay with his cousin Bill Dorling. My father was at work and to my mother's horror Billy Clements marched right into the house with his bag and his umbrella and sat down to wait for my father. My mother was sceptical. She knew my father's older brother lived in Buxton and would have known about his late wife as she died a year after I was born but my uncle had remarried in 1959 and no one had mentioned other Derbyshire relations. My father would not be back from work for several hours and so she parked him in the front room pending his return. I do not think she even offered him a cup of tea. She had never heard of his existence before this day and was certainly not going to accept his version of events without some corroboration. My parents always travelled around Ely on their bicycles and our terrace of houses had long passages at both ends of the terrace and there was a manhole cover about three-quarters of the way down the passage which rattled when they wheeled a bicycle over it. On hearing the rattle some hours after Billy Clements' arrival my mother, by now quite agitated, was able to intercept my father before he came into the house. There were some muffled negotiations by the back door before he came in to greet Billy who was indeed his cousin. Billy Clements was twenty years older than my father and I am not sure that they had met before although my father knew exactly who he was.

Once accepted as a bona fide relative Billy Clements was

CYRIL AND SARAH GOTHARD'S GRAVESTONE, WILBURTON

welcomed and invited for a meal. He was warm towards my mother and did not seem in any way surprised that she had not welcomed him on his arrival. In the evening he told us that as an infant he had lived with my father's parents, William and Rachel Dorling, and that he was the illegitimate son of my grandmother's older sister, Sarah Clements, who he believed had been in service at Hardwick Hall in Derbyshire. We knew Hardwick Hall because we had visited it once with my uncle and his second wife on a trip to Buxton. It is a grand Elizabethan country house built by Bess of Hardwick and many years later when I visited the house with my daughter the National Trust who owned it were calling for details of people who had worked below stairs for a forthcoming exhibition. I sent details of my great-aunt Sarah Clements but they did not reply so I assume that they could not confirm that she lived or worked there. By contrast details of all the servants employed at nearby Chatsworth House have been catalogued and are publicly available online. My great-aunts had all been in service from the age of thirteen so Billy Clements' story was likely to have been true but it was unlikely in those days that his mother would have discussed the manner of his conception and birth with him in any detail. She had died twenty years before his visit to us. Billy Clements thought his mother had had an affair with one of the sons of the house and that when she was in the late stages of pregnancy she had been dispatched by the family at their expense to London where Billy was born. Alternatively, he said, it was possible that his father was a clergyman because he knew his mother had married her husband, Billy Clements' step-father, Thomas Henderson, whilst living at a vicarage in Putney, South West London. As Billy's full name was William Massie Clements he was sure his father was a Mr Massie or perhaps had the Christian name of Massie.

My parents felt obliged to put Billy Clements up that night

MY FATHER, BILL
DORLING, IN 1937, AGED 19

while my father thought about what to do with him as it was clear from his luggage that he intended to stay in the area for some time and my mother did not want him to stay with us. I was thirteen at the time and I slept in the second bedroom at the front of the house but I was moved out of my bedroom and put back in the small box room off my parents' bedroom that I had slept in as a young child. The next day was a Saturday and my father, who was a general labourer for a local builders' firm called Tuckers, was only working in the morning, and he was under some pressure from my mother to move Billy Clements on. We did not have a car then, and no one we knew had telephones, but he managed to get a lift with his brother-in-law Vic in Tuckers' work van, that took the Soham workers home every Saturday lunchtime. He went to consult his sister Rose in Soham but when it was clear she would not take Billy in she drove him over to their sister Flo in Littleport but she also was reluctant to take Billy off our hands. They were nearer in age to Billy Clements and knew him from the past and in any case they said that he had chosen to come to us. Then a few days later the husband of the husband of another cousin of my father who also lived in Ely died suddenly and Billy saw an opportunity to move in with the widow. He packed his bag and without pre-warning his cousin moved in with her. This was Tot (Rhoda) Peacock, a blind woman and the daughter of another of my father's aunts, Hannah Clements, known as Nancy. Billy Clements taking up residence with her immediately after her husband's death and when funeral arrangements were being planned was not a good idea at all and the stay only lasted a few days because Billy sang loudly during the night which so unsettled Tot Peacock that she sent him straight back to us. He stayed with us for a few weeks and travelled around the Fens sight-seeing and making interesting purchases of small antiques which he would talk about in the evenings. He convinced my mother about a formula to reduce blood pressure and keep weight down made of cider apple vinegar and clear honey which she drank every night for the rest of her life so although we never saw Billy Clements again he was never forgotten.

Sarah Clements: Billy's Mother

In her teens, my grandmother Rachel's sister, Sarah Clements, had gone into service with a family in St Ives, a market town about 30 miles from Branch Bank, Prickwillow where the family were living at the time. She worked for a Corn Merchant and Brewer, Thomas Knights and his wife, as a general servant to the couple and their four adult children. Thomas Knights and his wife were both in their seventies. He was still working and his eldest son, in his early thirties, was working as a brewer for his father and the younger son was a florist. The daughters were older and not working. As the only servant in the house, and at the age of twenty, Sarah Clements would have done everything needed to keep the house serviced for the six people living there, and I imagine her day started early clearing the fireplace and fitting in the cleaning, shopping and laundry between preparing and serving meals. There is little information about what Sarah Clements was doing between working for the Knights family in St Ives in 1891 when she was twenty, and the birth of Billy Clements at Queen Charlotte's Hospital in London seven years later on November 12th 1898. Queen Charlotte's was a famous and well-established lying-in hospital then in the Marylebone Road which, unusually, took in both married and single women, although the latter for first babies only as young women were not expected to make the same mistake twice. After the birth Sarah Clements, by then twenty-seven, went to Leeds where she worked for a woollen merchant and his wife, the Dodgshuns, and their two daughters and where she is described as both a domestic cook and a god-daughter. There is little hard evidence that she was at Hardwick Hall but she must have lived in Derbyshire or had some contact with the area because in 1902 she married a man from Buxton. The marriage took place in Richmond in Surrey as Billy had said, and Sarah Clements was living there in the month before the wedding and gave her address as the vicarage of St John's church in Richmond, Surrey. The Banns were read for her fiancé, Thomas Henderson, in Buxton.

Sarah Clements became pregnant in the Spring of 1898, gave birth in London in November, and on Thursday, December 1st her son, William Massie Clements, was one of twenty babies baptised in the hospital chapel by the Rev G.C. Campbell and registered through St Mark's Church in the Marylebone Road. Fourteen of the babies, including twins, were born to single mothers. Sarah Clements' place of abode is given as the hospital. She must have stayed on in London for a few weeks after the birth and then travelled back to the Fens with the baby before Christmas probably staying with her sister, Hannah, and her husband Thomas Cross, who had been married for thirteen years and had a six year old daughter, Rhoda ('Tot') by then. They were living in Branch Bank,

Prickwillow, next door to their widowed father, William Clements whose wife, Mary, had died in June 1893 just before the birth of Hannah's daughter. Hannah Clements was five years older than his sister Sarah and had gone into service some years before her. Hannah Clements had been a general servant in the 1880s, and I have already mentioned her history.

My grandparents, William Dorling and Rachel Clements, married on 14th February 1899 and immediately afterwards Sarah Clements deposited her two-month-old baby, Billy, with them at their new home on the edges of Prickwillow where William Dorling was working as an agricultural labourer, and then Sarah went on to the Dodgshuns in Leeds where she worked for them as a cook, and from where she probably sent her sister money for the baby's upkeep. Three years later in February 1902 Sarah travelled from Leeds to Richmond in Surrey and stayed at the vicarage preparing for her marriage to Thomas Henderson, a carriage driver from Manchester who was working for the Livery Stables in Buxton at the time. By then my grandparents, Rachel and William Dorling had a child of their own, Victoria May (Lil, born in June 1901). Sarah Clements and her new husband, Thomas Henderson must have journeyed to Prickwillow soon after the wedding in Surrey to collect Billy Clements from my grandparents and take him with them to Buxton where they settled. Billy's step-sister Mabel, who would marry my uncle, was born in Chapel-le-frith, on 22 December 1902.

Sarah Clements went through a very difficult time from the time she discovered that she was pregnant but there is every indication that the family of the baby's father looked after her, paid her expenses and found her work. She probably never saw Billy's father again, but *someone* organised her stay at Queen Charlotte's Hospital, paid for her travel from Derbyshire to London and on to Leeds via the Fens, found her a position as a cook in Leeds where the family seems to have treated her as a relative, and made the connection with the vicarage in Surrey. Once married her minders seem to have faded into the distance, their responsibilities discharged.

CHAPTER 9

Maria Clements and Lambeth

We moved from Colchester in Essex to South London in 1986, just before my father died, to a large ground floor flat opposite Clapham Common. I had been working as Education Officer for the Royal Opera since 1983, the first such appointment, and already knew the London boroughs south of the river thanks to projects funded by the Inner London Education Authority (ILEA) in Covent Garden's four immediate neighbouring boroughs: Camden and Westminster north of the river, and Lambeth and Southwark to the south. I had lived in Bromley for three years when doing a teacher training course at Stockwell College in the early 1970s but rarely went into central London at that time. My first experience of being in London classrooms was a primary school in Creek Road, Deptford, which was then part of a special educational zone where teachers were paid higher rates because the area was classified as economically deprived. I had no concept at the time of urban poverty or what was then called 'multi-racial education', but the strangest thing to me, other than rabbits hopping in and out of the classrooms 'to develop empathy', was ITA, the Initial Teaching Alphabet, a simplified system of English intended to make teaching reading easier by using a quasi-phonetic alphabet, but breaking the first law of all pedagogical theory, because once mastered ITA had then to be unlearnt in order to learn standard English. As all the text books as well as the reading scheme books had been translated into ITA none of the student teachers could decipher them and we were not allowed to teach reading or writing, and could not use the books for other curriculum work either. Equally frustrating was my first proper teaching practice the following term in an affluent school on the edge of Bromley where the headteacher had devised his own method of teaching primary mathematics using Cuisenaire rods, and where only teachers trained in his way of using the coloured rods could teach maths. In consequence my first formal teaching experiences in primary schools debarred me from teaching reading, writing and maths, even though I had been trained up to teach basic reading as a sixth-former when I was assigned to Miss Goose at my old infant school as sixth-form work experience every Monday afternoon, and had been taught maths myself with Cuisenaire rods.

This was the heyday of progressive education building on the 1967 Plowden Report, *Children and their Primary Schools,* when primary school education put the learner at the centre of the curriculum and 'the task of the teacher', as illustrated to students at my college by a film of the same name shown from a reel-to-reel projector as part of our induction, was to encourage, curate and stimulate learning rather than to impart knowledge. My own infant school, St Audrey's in Ely, as said, was on this model and must have been a prototype for many of the ideas in Plowden. A local woman, Sybil Marshall (1913-2005), had developed a cross-curricula teaching approach to encourage children's creativity and the teaching of art in Cambridgeshire and her book, *An Experiment in Education* (1963), influenced Plowden and was on the syllabus in my first year of teacher training. (St Audrey's was named after the Abbess Aethelthryth or Etheldreda.) The school was purpose-built on a new campus on Downham Road on the site where my paternal grandparents had lived throughout their married life including during the second world war when they took in evacuees from London, and across the fields from my grammar school. It was a huge site of thirty-three acres owned by the Local Authority, and later in 1969 a secondary modern school was added. Needham's School was named after a local benefactress, Catherine Needham, who had died in 1730 and left funds to build and maintain a schools for 'poor boys in the city of Ely'. At St. Audrey's there was a single corridor with individual classrooms to the left overlooking a school field with a small hill where our annual May Day celebrations with maypoles and dancing were held, and cloakrooms to the right. All the children took part in the May Day event with each class forming its own circle to perform a special country dance. Girls were selected as the May Queen and her attendants if they could supply a suitable dress, and because I had been a bridesmaid at my cousin's wedding I was selected one May Day as an attendant and wore a long red velvet dress and a white feathery coronet from the wedding. At the far end was a school hall for assembly, lunch and arts activities. Classrooms were organised with workstations with inviting educational tasks and all had floor to ceiling windows on one side and so were full of light. It was a perfect educational setting, completely out-of-step with the Victorian-style junior school which was to follow and where all but those whose parents could afford the only available private alternative would go to at the end of the two years. St Audrey's was indicative of the ambition that Cambridgeshire Local Authority had had since the 1930s which included the creation of Village Colleges, the brainchild of Henry Morris (1889-1961) as Chief Executive. He saw schools as community hubs located in inspirational buildings. Impington Village College, where I later ran an opera project for the Royal Opera, opened in 1939 in a building designed by the famous architect and Bauhaus founder,

IMPINGTON VILLAGE COLLEGE, CAMBRIDGESHIRE

Walter Gropius, and is the only example of his work in the UK. My own infant school was obviously inspired by his design.

By 1983 when I started working with ILEA schools, some of the more experimental pedagogy had disappeared but there was still huge ambition for Inner London's students. ILEA had enormous budgets which beyond the schools themselves funded teams of additional staff employed to run theatre, music, film and visual arts programmes for the Authority with a remit to commission professional arts organisations like the Royal Opera. They even funded and ran two museums: the Geffrye Museum in Shoreditch and the Horniman in Forest Hill. I ran opera projects with artists in many London schools in inner London when the ILEA still funded activity before Margaret Thatcher's dismantling of the ILEA in 1990. I visited almost all the secondary schools and many primaries in Lambeth and Southwark. I did not realise at the time that the schools I visited in Lambeth and Southwark in the 1980s were in many of the streets that my great-great aunt, Maria Clements, the daughter of Rhoda Francis Clements, would have known when she moved to London in the 1850s.

North Lambeth 1850s

Maria Clements was living with her parents in Branch Bank in 1851 when she was seventeen. There were four younger children and an older brother who was working as a farm labourer and living with their parents, Rhoda and John Clements. Her other older siblings, Mary, James and Samuel Clements had left home for positions as live-in servants and my great-grandfather William Clements, two years younger than Maria, was working as an agricultural labourer and in lodgings in another part of the Prickwillow Fen. It is hard to imagine why Maria Clements went to London when she did. She would certainly have been under pressure to find a paid position from the age of thirteen and so very probably had had at least one live-in job as a servant locally before moving back to her parents' home briefly and then leaving for London. Had she ready found employment in London somehow? Did she know someone there? Did she decide to travel to London speculatively but confident of finding a position? Was she running away? Her parents' expectation would have been that she would settle down and marry a local man and stay in the Fens.

Maria Clements may have been more ambitious than many local girls because sometime between 1851 and 1853 she travelled to London and ended up in Lambeth on the south side of the River Thames. The railway station in Ely had opened in 1845 but more likely Maria Clements travelled by coach. We know that from the eighteenth century there was a mail coach that left Market Street and that almost certainly Maria Clements would have taken a coach that would have concluded its journey at La Belle Sauvage, a coaching inn in Ludgate Hill in the City of London (demolished in 1873 for the building of Holborn Viaduct). We do not know if she made straight for Lambeth from there or whether she spent time north of the river first. If I had little concept of London life when I moved there from Ely in 1973 how much more of a challenge would it have been for Maria Clements in the mid-1850s with her only experience being of Cambridgeshire and its flat agricultural land, its farm labourers and her parents' isolated house on the banks of the River Lark? Although I had never stayed in London I had at least been there, for a school trip to Kew Gardens, to see the Royal Shakespeare Company's production of *A Midsummer Night's Dream*, the famous one by Peter Brook at the Aldwych Theatre in 1970 just before my English Literature 'O' level examination, or with my parents on a sightseeing trip when we were hosting my French penpals.

Ely at the time was growing and the railway building in the area meant that its station was a junction for three railway lines. Maria Clements may have been aware of this, and of an area on Lynn Road which was particularly poor and dubbed 'Little London'. There were 1552 houses in the city in 1848 and half were sub-standard. People were living in poverty with a poor diet and poor ventilation and using open ditches for sewage. Mortality rates were high, particularly for babies and small children. But the Lambeth Maria Clements went to was in the middle of even more rapid population growth following the establishment of the railways there. Slums were still to be cleared, new roads to be built and the construction of the Albert Embankment would not start until 1865. Along the road the Vauxhall Pleasure Gardens were still in operation but would be closed in 1859. Lambeth Palace was the major landmark, the London home of the Archbishop of Canterbury since the twelfth century with the main parish church, St Mary, adjacent at the foot of Lambeth Bridge, now the Garden Museum. One common feature with the Fens was that the area had been a swamp for much of its history with some buildings erected on stilts to cope with the river flooding that was a regular feature until the later drainage improvements. There were warehouses along the length of the river front from Lambeth

Palace to Deptford Creek. The area had breweries, chemical works, soap and candle makers, steam engine works and was well-known for its potteries and stone works. Houses were heated with coal fires which were also used for cooking causing the area to be dark and smoky.

In 1855 the ad hoc arrangements for managing London's settlements were replaced by the establishment of the Metropolitan Board of Works which had London-wide responsibility for addressing issues associated with London's rapid growth. Maria Clements arrived in Lambeth before the Board-initiated infrastructural developments including the creation of sewers. Two of Maria's cousins, Rhoda Clements' nephews Fincham and Jacob Francis, would move with a group of Littleport men to West Ham in the early 1860s to work on Joseph Bazalgette's sewerage schemes. Thousands of labourers moved into London from all over the country and from Ireland to dig manually the new sewers as part of the London project commissioned after the 'Great Stink' of 1858. Jacob Francis settled in West Ham and never returned to Littleport.

New factories had grown up along the two miles of Lambeth that lined the River Thames with houses being speedily erected for the influx of workers. At the time of the 1841 census the population of the area had grown to 130,000 from 34,000 in 1801, and by the time Maria arrived it was nearer 160,000 with little infrastructure to support the recent growth. Migrant workers for the factories were crammed into temporary buildings. Occupants drew their household water from the same river which was operating as a sewage route which proved fatal when the cholera epidemic struck the area in 1848-49 killing nearly two thousand residents. Today the epidemic is commemorated with a memorial and a plaque on the south bank of the Thames opposite Tate Britain and I often passed it on my route from my office at Arts Council England in Great Peter Street, walking from the north across Lambeth Bridge and along the Albert Embankment to Vauxhall Station in the early 2000s. When Maria Clements arrived in Lambeth the Tate site on the north of the river would have housed the Millbank Prison which in 1843 had been downgraded from being the National Penitentiary to become a holding depot for prisoners destined for transportation to Australia. It is possible that Maria's older brother, James Clements, last seen in the Fens in 1843 and definitely out of the country by 1851, may have been one of the first such condemned men to start his sentence at Millbank Prison before being transported to Botany Bay.

1848 was the year in which the original Waterloo station was built, extending the London and South West railway from Nine Elms and cutting off streets from the river, creating impoverished cul-de-sacs. Maria Clements moved into the area four or five years after the building of the station by which time it was a crowded area of tenements, factories, public houses and gin shops. Anything more contrasted to the isolation of Branch Bank is hard to imagine and whereas all the people she would have known in Cambridgeshire would have all been farmers and labourers, here she would have encountered barge builders, shopkeepers, blacksmiths, rag-and-bone men, glove makers, laundresses, bookbinders and warehouse men all packed together in tiny houses.

The Woosters

Maria Clements married Charles Wooster, a chair-maker, in 1854 when she was twenty, in St Mary the Less Church which was in what is now Black Prince Road, very near where the Cholera Memorial is today. It had been built as a chapel of ease for St Mary Lambeth and became a parish in its own right in the 1870s. Charles' father George Wooster was also a chair-maker and came from High Wycombe, probably attracted to London because wages were higher

MEMORIAL FOR THE CHOLERA EPIDEMIC (1848-1849) ON WHITE HART DOCK, ALBERT EMBANKMENT, NEAR BLACK PRINCE ROAD, LAMBETH.

than in the country. High Wycombe was a chair-making centre in the nineteenth century famous for its Windsor chairs. High Wycombe chair-makers supplied major national events at the time including royal weddings, and in 1873 19,200 chairs were provided to the American evangelists, Moody and Sankey, for their big rallies at the Islington Agricultural Hall, now the Business Design Centre on Upper Street. George Wooster's work would have been mostly woodwork and carpentry, making chair frames, legs, arms and backs. He almost certainly had no role in upholstering chairs which would have required expensive fabrics and a different set of skills but he would probably have supplied middle-men with frames for selling on. He would have needed space in the house for a workshop and would have had specialist tools but the skill of chair-making was considered to be at the lowly end of the crafts, far short of cabinet-making or fine carving. Logically the expansion of the City would suggest a greater need for chairs, but with child labour, agencies under-cutting craftsmen, and the fact that once a chair-maker had expended money on materials and made a chair his need to 'convert' the finished product into ready cash for food and lodgings was urgent and he often had to take lower prices or indeed sell to the 'Slaughterhouses' who, as agencies without the same cash-flow problems, could drive down prices. Making a living in the chair business became a downward spiral for individual makers, and contemporary reports suggesting that wages decreased for chair-makers by some 300% over the century.

The Windsor chair is plain wooden, slotted together from pre-made parts, and with a chair back that is completely separate from the seat and legs – Ercol chairs which were first created as part of the Utility Furniture Scheme (UFS) were similar and have become very sought after again. [The government guaranteed cheap timber in rationing times, from 1942 to 1949, for 'utility' furniture.] My parents had mostly Utility Scheme furniture in my childhood which my mother replaced as soon as she could often with more fashionable but poorer quality items. When she moved from the family home in 1994 she still owned two UFS wardrobes, a large one for the woman of the house and a smaller matching men's wardrobe, and a dressing table with two sets of drawers, a drop-down central glass shelf and large mirror which were all still as new. Having married in 1948 just after the war my parents would have been entitled to use the UFS scheme.

Maria's father-in-law, had been born in Hughenden near High Wycombe to a single mother and he trained to be a chair-maker there and then moved to Lambeth in early adulthood where he met and married a widow, Sarah Stubbs, in 1821. Sarah Stubbs had a son, John, from her earlier marriage and George Wooster taught his step-son the chair-making trade as well as training his own two sons, George and Charles Wooster. Sarah was a French Polisher, but both she and Maria were taught to cane chairs and considered themselves primarily chair-caners. When the sons were older, the three Wooster households were all making and selling chairs from their homes presumably to retailers, with the wives and daughters working as chair caners, but also training the sons as soon as they were ten years old as there were a number of discrete activities which could be farmed out to children or less-skilled workers, such as wood-chopping and making chair legs. There was a wider cluster of families working as chair-makers in the 1850s living in adjacent houses in Barrett Street at the north end of what is now Vauxhall Street near Venn Park in North Lambeth and a few minutes' walk from the river. As well as the Woosters, (George and his two sons) there was John Stubbs and his wife Elizabeth, the Abbots, the Chapmans and the Sorrells all living in the Barrett Street.

Charles Wooster was about nine years older than Maria Clements, although his dates are not certain and are recorded differently over the years, as is his birth-place which on one census is recorded as Brecon in Wales, while his name is given as Richard in another place, but in all cases it is unmistakably him. On her marriage Maria moved in with Charles Wooster and his father George, by now widowed, in Barrett Street, very near the Lambeth Workhouse in Princes' Road where George would die. They worked hard long hours -probably twelve-hour days – but the craft was not well remunerated and there was no prospect of saving for luxuries or for retirement: in 1911, aged seventy-seven, Maria Wooster described herself in the census as 'Chair caner – unable to work', and her father-in-law George Wooster is listed as a chair-maker during his final days in the Prince's Road workhouse. Charles and Maria Wooster's circumstances were very poor from the start of their marriage and the arrival of children compounded their problems. Their first child, Maria, was born in 1855 and was baptised at St Mary the Less (Black Prince Road, now destroyed) in April 1859 at the age of four and the occasion was almost certainly prompted by the death of their second child, Rhoda whom they buried unbaptised earlier that year, aged three. A third child, Eliza, was born while they were in Barrett Street.

In 1862 Maria and Charles Wooster moved south from Lambeth to Southwark finding accommodation in Artichoke Place near Camberwell Green in South London, at the junction of Grove Lane and Camberwell Church Street, leaving Charles' father George Wooster in North Lambeth to give up the home he had shared with Charles and Maria, and move in with his other son. Charles and Maria Wooster must have decided that there were too many chair-makers in Barrett Street and that to survive with their growing family they needed to branch out and find a new place of business.

In the years between 1861 and 1869 Maria Wooster gave birth to five more children including George in 1862 who probably died soon after birth as there is no record of his baptism. On Sunday, 14 March 1869 four Wooster boys, Charles (aged 7), James (5), George John (2) and William (1) were baptised together at St Giles Church in Camberwell Church Street, just a few steps away from where they were living. St Giles had been consecrated in 1844 and was the first 'Gothic' church built by Gilbert Scott between 1841 and 1844, replacing a medieval church which had been destroyed by fire. (Scott would go on supervise the refurbishment of Ely Cathedral, the first of the English cathedrals to be renovated in the nineteenth century.) Eliza Wooster, Maria's third daughter died in April 1869, aged nine. In 1871 there were five children under eight in the household as well as oldest daughter Maria Wooster, by now aged fifteen and described as an unemployed domestic servant so she had almost certainly had at least one servant position by this point.

Maria Wooster would have been ill-prepared for urban poverty which, as well as poor living conditions, brought all the additional city health challenges associated with over-crowded housing, including the prevalence of infectious diseases, and for the poor no access to medical services. Unlike Maria Wooster's siblings who had all found employment away from home from the age of thirteen as servants or as agricultural labourers none of Maria's own children seemed to be able to hold down long-term sustainable work in Southwark, and none were able to work as chair-makers presumably because demand for chairs had dried up or because the financial margins had become so tight.

Beckett Street, Camberwell 1870s

In the mid-1870s Charles and Maria Wooster moved the family again, this time to Beckett Street in Camberwell, one of a notorious cluster of streets in Camberwell, now gone, which also included Sultan Street, Hollington Street, Crown Street, Gange Street, and Toulon Street, known for high levels of poverty and located between the Camberwell and New Camberwell roads, blocked off by the new railway lines. Maria Wooster, her children and her friends lived in this block of streets after the 1870s. Unlike her mother who saw most of her children move far away from the family often to find better lives, Maria Wooster held her children close and none of them ever lived more than a couple of streets away from their mother, and Maria's door was always open to them because, over the years, she took them back in as adults when they needed a roof or were out of work. The area is marked dark blue in Charles Booth's Poverty Maps suggesting it was known for semi-criminal activity. In 1895 there were numerous reports and responses between the Medical Officer of Health for Camberwell and the Vestry in which we read about long-term issues with these streets: 'The overcrowding in this district and the sad state in which the inhabitants have for many years been compelled to subsist have been a source of the deepest pain to the clergy and others brought into contact with the poor people dwelling in this neglected area. In many of the houses five or six families reside, and scores of instances can be shown where a family (sometimes embracing several adults of both sexes) exist in a single room.' It continues that many of the dwellings housed five or six families, with families living in a single room and that the 'neighbourhood is a black spot in the midst of a comparatively well-to-do, well-ordered Parish. It is, as it were, shut in with its vice and wretchedness, having practically no thoroughfare connecting it with the main roads'. The writers talk of the area as a 'moral cesspool', 'the despair of the clergy' with the residents 'continually shifting'. The Chief Medical Officer writing the report felt there had been some exaggeration of the poor conditions, particularly in Beckett Street, where Charles and Maria Wooster lived, and where it had been claimed that people kept donkeys in their houses. He replied that 'in the whole of Beckett Street I found but one instance [of people keeping donkeys in their houses]…that the donkey was only there temporarily' but that it was definitely the cases that donkeys kept in the back yards had to be taken to the street via the living areas 'but we are met by this fact, that if we do not allow the people to keep donkeys under these conditions we are practically doing away with their means of livelihood'. Two of Maria Wooster's sons were rag-pickers, or rag-and-bone men and could perhaps have had a donkey, although more probably Edward and James Wooster would have been men who went out onto the streets on foot early each morning, for nine or ten hours a day with a small bag on their backs scavenging rags, bone and metal for salvage. At the end of the day they would sort through what they found and sell what they could to collectors, often ex-rag-pickers themselves, who in turn could sell on to traders who knew how to translate the items into a profit. Although an honest-enough occupation, they were probably perceived as very lowly and perhaps attracted the ire and abuse of neighbours. The amount of money thus raised would have been meagre, and it seems probable that Edward and James both had health issues throughout their lives and would have had long periods when they were unable to work at all.

The roadways, continued the Camberwell reports, were dirty, and the 'cleansing of the street…made impossible by the fact that the costermongers' barrows are stored in it.' There were more than four and a half thousand people living in these six or seven tightly-packed streets at the time, which became a political football with pressure to demolish the whole area on the one hand and resistance to change on the other on the grounds that if the poor lost what livelihoods they had, they would become poorer, and thus more dependent on the Vestry [i.e. the local church parish office, which until 1900 had responsibility for the poor]. The houses were back-to-back; sometimes if lucky a family would have two rooms plus a washhouse. Poor ventilation caused the floors to rot, and the walls to be damp. There were water-closets in the back yards with the 'stables' accessed through the houses. These were the conditions for Maria Wooster and her family. In 1881 eleven of them were living together in Beckett Street, probably in two damp rooms: Maria and Charles with nine children aged between three and twenty-six years old. The older children were variously factory workers, wood-choppers and labourers. Around the corner their friends, Richard and Alice Foord in Sultan Street were living, we assume, in similar conditions although Foord, who grew up in neighbouring Hollington Street had epilepsy, and episodes of 'fits' are given as reasons for the admission of Foord and his young family into the Constance Road and Gordon Road workhouses on several occasions in the late 1890s, with at least one admittance coinciding with that of Maria Wooster's son James. Two of Foord's children died in early childhood and Foord's wife died at the age of forty-seven. It is hard not to conclude that they were ground down by being in the workhouses and living hand-to-mouth in different housing arrangements outside.

GORDON ROAD WORKHOUSE TODAY

Camberwell, 1880s

In 1886 Charles Wooster died leaving Maria Wooster a widow and forcing another house move to nearby Waterloo Street near Camberwell Green in what is now Elmington Road, just north of Church Street and the Camberwell Arms. Their daughter Amelia Wooster had work as a live-in work domestic servant in Denmark Hill in one of the streets opposite King's College Hospital and perhaps thought life was taking a positive turn, but as a fifteen year-old girl working as the sole domestic servant to a commercial clerk and his family, her life would have been hard. The couple she worked for had five children between the ages of seven months and fifteen, and the house in Denmark Hill was a large one on three floors. Hours would have been long and life could not have been easy but at least she was away from home and not dependent on her widowed mother's limited means. None of Maria Wooster's children had married at this time and their jobs were all precarious, much like the zero hours contracts of today with long hours and without any guarantee of work or pay. Maria Wooster must have been doing all in her power to keep her children out of the workhouses. Unfortunately from the late 1880s onwards Maria Wooster, her children, her father-in-law, and their friends and neighbours lost this battle and became frequent inmates of the Southwark and Lambeth workhouses.

We have often walked around Camberwell and there are two striking buildings that have recently been re-purposed as flats. These are the Camberwell workhouses which took in the poor, infirm and insane from the 1830s onwards. My daughter once lived at the Nunhead Green end of Gordon Road and a short walk away there was number 20 Gordon Road which had been the 'new' Camberwell workhouse built in 1878 for 743 able-bodied inmates with the men required to work as stone-breakers or wood choppers, and the women as laundry workers. The original Camberwell workhouse was in Havil Street and built in 1818 as a long, narrow building on two storeys with a basement. Contemporary reports in *The Lancet* suggest it was lacking in most respects and badly staffed. In 1889 a distinctive circular tower-

HAVIL ROAD WORKHOUSE TODAY

like building was added fronting onto Havil Road and it was extended again in 1899. The latest of the three workhouses was in Constance Road in East Dulwich which accommodated 1000 inmates who were mostly infirm or 'lunatic', and what remains of it has been incorporated within Dulwich Hospital.

It is hard to keep track of Maria Wooster's family. If we take a snapshot in 1901 when Maria Wooster was sixty-seven and had been a widow for five years and advertising herself in Kelly's Directory as a chair-caner operating from 75 Waterloo Street in Camberwell, six of her thirteen children had died including Charles who died that year, aged 39, in Havil Street workhouse where he had been living for two years. Her surviving children are either living with her or in the immediate vicinity. Maria, her eldest, still single, is in lodgings around the corner from her mother in Picton Street, and still working as a charwoman. Four children, George, 39, William, 33, Amelia, 31 and Edward, 29 are back living with their mother, all single and doing menial jobs. Richard, 23, Maria's youngest boy, now known as Samuel, had married two years earlier in 1899 and was living with his wife and their nine-month old baby daughter nearby. Like Charles, James Wooster had a long-term history of sickness and was 'a pauper inmate' in Gordon Road Workhouse where he would die within months. Presumably Maria's circumstances were not suitable for keeping her sickly adult children at home.

Amelia Wooster, temporarily unemployed had gone back to her mother's house in 1901 but managed to find a post as a servant in Brixton Hill soon after and in 1907 she became pregnant while working there, giving birth, aged 37 to Amelia Wooster Horsman. She married the baby's father, William Horsman, in 1909, around the time of the birth of a son, Alfred Horsman. William Horsman was a widower with five children of his own. From the time of the marriage Amelia Horsman was in and out of Westmoreland

Road workhouse living a complicated life which involved farming out her children and step-children to relatives and friends around the area to keep them out of the workhouse. The Westmoreland workhouse was located between the Old Kent and Walworth roads and had originally been planned as an industrial school but was never used as such being re-purposed as a building 'to house adult paupers'. In the twentieth century the building was used as short-term accommodation for homeless people and featured in Ken Loach's *Cathy Come Home* television play by the BBC in 1966 in the series called 'The Wednesday Play' which I remember watching with my parents. (The charity Shelter was created at around the same time and the shock caused by the programme helped publicise it.) My parents loved watching television documentaries about social conditions and current affairs and *Panorama, World in Action, Man Alive* were never missed, all painting a very bleak picture of working-class lives and, as my parents read them, examples of the exploitation of working people by the ruling classes, or as my mother would say, 'the idle rich'.

On 8 November 1911 Amelia Horsman gave birth to another daughter, Louisa, in the Westmoreland Road Workhouse, and the mother and baby were 'discharged to William Horsman'. In August 1912 the whole family, William, Amelia, then 41, along with Ada 10, William's daughter, Amelia, 5, Alfred 3, and Louisa 1 were all back in the workhouse through 'lack of means'. This pattern would continue for the rest of their lives.

Maria's oldest daughter, Maria Wooster, would make a late marriage in 1913 at the age of fifty-eight (although both parties gave their ages as younger for the purpose of the banns), to their family friend, Richard Foord who had been widowed nine years earlier. From the time of his first wife's death Foord lived in Manor House Chambers at 124, Camberwell Road which was a common lodging house for 170 men managed by a manager, his wife and four servants. Although licensed by the Council Manor House Chambers was little better than a workhouse. Known as a dosshouse and sleeping several men to a room often with men using beds in shifts and paying by the day, or even by the hour, its only advantage over the workhouse was that the men were independent and not required to contribute their labour as stone cutters. Foord stayed in the 6d per day boarding house for more than five years and only left when he married Maria Wooster in 1913.

On 25 August 1917 Maria Clements Wooster was herself admitted into Constance Road workhouse in East Dulwich, not for the first time because we know that she and her son Samuel had been there at least once before, but this was to be the last time. From there on 1 September she was transferred to the Bexley Asylum having been diagnosed with cerebal softening, possibly caused by a stroke. She died in the Asylum in the October and was buried in Old Camberwell cemetery in an unmarked grave on 6 November 1917. Of her thirteen children Maria, George, Amelia, Edward and Samuel survived her. Samuel died in 1918, George in 1922, Amelia Horsman died in 1924 having lived a long and impoverished life in and out of workhouses and their infirmaries for the last fourteen years of her life. She was buried in Nunhead Cemetery. Edward Wooster died in 1933.

My granddaughter's first nursery was in Brockley Way, a Sure Start Centre set up by the Blair Labour Government in what is becoming a popular area in South East London. The quickest route from the nursery to my daughter's flat in Gordon Road was straight through the Nunhead Cemetery. Nunhead Cemetery is one of London's 'Magnificent Seven' Victorian cemeteries which ringed London. Nunhead Cemetery was originally called All Saints Cemetery and was consecrated in 1840. Camberwell Old Cemetery was built in Forest Hill later as part of a need to expand the available land for cemeteries in Camberwell. Maria and Charles Wooster and all but one of their children – little Rhoda was buried in Lambeth cemetery in January 1859 aged three – were buried in unmarked graves in Nunhead and Camberwell Old Cemeteries. Little did I know as I pushed a buggy through the graveyard that so many of my relatives were buried nearby.

Ely 1906

It seems unlikely that Maria Clements Wooster ever returned to the Fens and we do not know whether she heard about the death of her father, John Clements, in 1861, or that her brother Samuel was part of the American Civil War and died there in 1863, or what happened to James in Australia. Her time in the workhouse leading to her death in 1917 was short. Her older sister Mary King's demise was as sad. She was widowed in 1881,

ELY WORKHOUSE NOW FLATS BUT WHICH BECAME THE TOWER HOSPITAL WHERE MY FATHER BILL DORLING WORKED

her two surviving sons having already left the area to make new lives in America and Yorkshire and her daughter having died, so she had to admit herself to the Ely Workhouse from 1901 and there she died, 'King, Mary, 88, of the workhouse' in 1906. The Ely Workhouse has recently been converted into residential flats – now Tower Court – but from 1948 with the founding of the National Health Service it became a hospital – the Tower Hospital for elderly people. Built in 1836-7 its administrative block on three storeys resembled a castle and the workhouse was built to accommodate three hundred inmates. By 1939 it had become a 'Public Assistance Institution' then listing nearly 150 'inmates'. My father's last job before retirement in the 1970s was as a hospital porter there. I am sure he never knew that his great-aunt Mary had died in that building.

CHAPTER 10

Ely High School for Girls – and more clues

Although Cambridgeshire and the Isle of Ely were separate local authorities until 1965 the educational policies in Ely must have built on the work in wider Cambridgeshire where Educational Administrator, Henry Morris, had pioneered the concept of village colleges in the area immediately around Cambridge in the 1920s and 1930s. After the First World War the rural areas around Cambridge were some of the poorest places in the country. Morris saw that secondary schooling in the city of Cambridge was good but the neighbouring villages were emptying, and education was delivered through old-fashioned 5-14 elementary schools like the ones my parents attended in East Cambridgeshire. In Ely and its surrounding villages the poverty must have gone on for much longer. Henry Morris had realised that the normal practice in the villages was for boys to leave school for farm work and girls to work in service as my parents had done. Over thirty years in the county Henry Morris established a cluster of village colleges which were community education centres promoting life-long learning, comprising healthcare, village libraries, cultural and social activities for local people, and designed to reinvigorate village communities. By the 1960s the concept had proven successful and Isle of Ely village colleges were set up in Littleport, Witchford and Soham with a similar ethos. When the Isle of Ely adopted the comprehensive system in 1972 the building housing the girls' high school became the sixth form for the three local village colleges and the City of Ely College which all, to some extent, maintained their village college spirit of serving the whole community.

My two years at St Audrey's Infant school were very happy but in September 1962 we were transferred to the Ely junior school which was the exact opposite of an enlightened educational establishment. Colour in the form of lush green fields all around was replaced by a very grey mid-Victorian building in a plain street in the city centre around the corner from St Mary's Church. The main single storey building had two wings with separate entrances and a playground each for boys and girls. There were additional buildings at the back of the playground which had been built at the turn of the twentieth century with an outside toilet block between the original school and its extensions. The main building had school halls with classrooms on the street side. To cater for school lunches the school used a local British Legion hall which was adjacent. Officially the school was St Mary's Church of England Junior School and it had been formed by amalgamating a girls' school in Broad Street opposite the entrance to Ely Park, and the boys' school in Silver Street, but it was still universally known as Silver Street school. In my time at the school the Broad Street site functioned as an annexe where we would be decanted for the third year (what we would now call Y5). Because it was physically removed from the headteacher who never visited, it was a slightly more enlightened regime than in the main school with three benevolent male teachers. There was a school hall, office and classroom in the main building, and two classrooms in two 'demountables' built after the second world war. It later became a pottery and then, following a fire and renovation, a residential building. For years 1,2 and 4 we were based in the Silver Street site.

Just as St Audrey's had been a foretaste of mid-1970s child-centred education in primary colours embracing 'learning by doing' so St Mary's harked back to the 1950s and Victorian times in everything it did. On our first day at the school we gathered in the girls' playground. A teacher with a clipboard called out names and those called were taken off to a classroom at the front of the school where they were joined by an equivalent number of boys – forty-four children in total in what was class 1A. The school was three-form entry and strictly streamed with an A, B and C class in every year group. There were fewer children in the B and C forms. The classrooms were austere. There was a huge cast iron heating stove towards the front of each classroom on the left that heated those immediately around it but not the rest. Because we were allocated desks according to test results at the end of each year after the first year I managed to be located near the heater by dint of ranking somewhere between 5th and 9th in the class. When I was in the second year I had taken in a half-farthing to show the class. My father had been working for Tucker's on a demolition job and brought the coin home along with an old piano that he thought I might like. My parents must have told me the coin was very valuable so I was distraught when I lost it and was allowed to stay in over the playtime to search for it – it turned up under the huge stove. Desks were wooden and paired with two children sitting side by side. There were ceramic ink-wells and we learned to write with very basic fountain or 'dip' pens which were nibs with a wooden handle or holder. We worked through booklets of Marion Richardson handwriting patterns most days which I've since learnt that Richardson produced as part of her child-centred drawing and writing methods. The desks had lift-up lids. The teacher sat at the front and we seldom moved from our places other than when called up one by one to read to the teacher. Towards the end of each year each child was called up individually to do the Schonell reading age test with the teacher. The teacher had a card of words starting with short words in large letters at the top and getting progressively more complicated and smaller, rather like an Optician's chart, towards the bottom. After five errors the teacher stopped the test and was able to calculate a reading age which became the main feature of the bi-annual report to parents which would record the child's chronological age and reading age. In the second year we were allowed to rearrange the desks by pushing three desks together to accommodate six children with the better readers teaching the others.

The rest of the curriculum was limited to working through maths, 'comprehension exercises books along with live BBC broadcasts for music ('Singing Together') Science, and 'Nature'. For the latter we were often asked to bring in small items such as leaves or string as there was usually a practical making exercise involved. 'Singing together' was very popular as we had singing books issued by the BBC and learnt six or seven not-always-age-appropriate traditional songs from across the UK nations as well as sea shanties and carols.

The headmaster still used a cane to discipline the boys and teachers routinely hit them with rulers both for misdeeds and poor work. Girls were never struck but it was painful to watch a small boy walk towards his punishment at the front of the class with tears of anticipation in his eyes.

The sense of general discomfort was not helped by the fact that in 1963 the UK experienced its coldest winter ever – what was called the 'Big Freeze'. In the January-February period it was bitterly cold, and everything was covered with heavy snow. The crates of free milk, small bottles of a third of a pint of milk for every child, sat on the school doorstep with frozen cream popping out with their silver foil bottle tops on top. Exceptionally that year school buses were put on to transport children from the edges of Ely but we froze while waiting and it would have been better to have walked to school in the snow. We were used to the winter cold: few of us had heating in our houses other than a coal fire in the sitting room (my bedroom regularly had ice on the inside of the windows).

Those of us in the A stream progressed through the years – there was no movement between the streams – until in 4A our eyes were directed to the Eleven-plus examination. For most of the school year we worked through past papers of maths, English and verbal reasoning tests until we were proficient. I hardly remember the examination itself but some weeks later an official letter arrived from the Local Authority offering me a place at the Girls' Grammar school. The letter itself was very formal, hard to understand because it cited various bits of legislation, and there was a clause that girls accepting a place would have to commit to stay until the age of sixteen and that the uniform requirements were demanding.

> *Dear Sir or Madam*
> *The above-named child has been selected on the results of the recent Entrance Examination for admission to the above-named School at the commencement of the Autumn Term, 1966, that is, in September next.*
> *There will be no fees to pay.*
> *As a result of the Education Act, 1944, the Education Committee cannot award maintenance allowances in respect of children attending Secondary Schools until after the end of the school term in which they attain the age of 15 years.*

[............]
If you decide to send your child to the above-named school, the Education Committee will expect you to KEEP HER AT THAT SCHOOL UNTIL AT LEAST THE END OF THE SCHOOL YEAR IN WHICH SHE WILL ATTAIN THE AGE OF 16 YEARS.

A grammar school offer was unexpected. My father was surprised, but quietly pleased and proud. My mother found this development very challenging and was embarrassed and concerned that when the news broke, we would be accused of putting on airs. Her instinct was to keep the information quiet and she forbade me to tell anyone including my aunts and uncles. Luckily no one asked. In common with many working class children at the time the event marked a permanent change in the relationship between my mother and me.

Ely High School for Girls was founded in 1905 as a fee-paying secondary school for girls with a mixed preparatory school, the latter drawing on an earlier institution and closing in 1949. The school was housed in what must have been a very unsuitable building in St Mary's Street, built as a three-storey townhouse and called Bedford House after 1824 because it had been the offices of the Bedford Level Corporation for twenty years. This was the organisation that had been responsible for the drainage of the fens and, as well as a board room and offices, was the home of the organisation's registrar. The coat of arms for the Corporation was above the main door with its motto, Arridet Arridum' which translates as 'Dryness pleaseth'. What must have been a fine private house with handsome gardens probably functioned acceptably in the early years when student numbers were below 100 but, as numbers grew, the site was soon 'cluttered with wooden huts', temporary classrooms and old army huts, as the number of girls increased year on year. During the war years the school took in students from the Central Foundation School in Bishopsgate who were evacuated from East London. My father's parents, whose children had all left home by then, took in two girls as boarders, Freda and Marceline Sargeantson who were seven and twelve at the beginning of World War II. By 1944 there were 455 students on roll.

Following the 1944 Education Act the school became part of the national tri-partite system operating as a girls' grammar school and complementing provision for boys at Soham's much older grammar school. In 1957 a new building on Downham Road, was opened. Unlike its predecessor the new building was modern and light inside, and surrounded by fields providing spaces or outdoor games. The secondary modern school, Needham's named after Catherine Needham, a widow who had died in 1730 and left funds to set up an educational trust (which still exists), and which was located in a school building on Back Hill, until its own relocation to a new building on the Downham Road site in 1969.

There must have been a desire to instil some traditions into the new school. Four 'houses' established in the 1920s celebrated local heroes. There was Etheldreda House, named after St Etheldreda – also known as St Audrey – who founded an abbey in Ely in 673. Knut house was named after the 11th century king who was known to have a fondness for Ely and its abbey. Alan was Alan of Walsingham who supervised the construction of Ely Cathedral's famous Octagon Tower when an earlier Norman tower collapsed in 1322. My house was Hereward: Hereward the Wake, the rebel who held out against the Normans approaching the Isle of Ely. The school's motto 'Fortiter ad Fastigium' which was part of our school badge which had to be sewn onto our blazer pockets, berets and boaters translated as 'Bravely to the Top' and was a later piece of 'tradition' added when the school moved to its new building in

Ely High School for Girls – and more clues

Downham Road and was inspired by Hilary and Tensing's ascent of Mount Everest in 1953. There was a school hymn, 'O God whose light glows in the golden sunshine…' which in the mid-1960s was a lively song sung at pace, accompanied by an inspirational music teacher called Miss Greenwood. I was surprised to hear the same hymn at the centenary event in 2005 where it was more of a dirge and not inspiring at all. By the time of the centenary, which was a thanksgiving service in Ely Cathedral's Lady Chapel, the school had been closed for more than thirty years, having been subsumed within the new comprehensive arrangements in the 1970s.

Coda and Acknowledgements
(Jeremy Tambling)

Ely the city ends suddenly in all directions and becomes flat black farmland, towards Littleport to the north, Soham and Stuntney to the south and Prickwillow and Witchford to east and west. Driving through the Fens one is aware of other settlements and villages that are slightly higher than the surrounding land, reaching as far as Norfolk, Suffolk and Lincolnshire. It is countryside but not green, or 'rolling' or with dry stone walls or sheep. It is 'land' not 'fields' and flat and black. Outside the City farmland stretches to the very edges of the road with a ditch or dyke dividing the road from the land. No paths. Throughout the Fen there are rivers, drains and dykes but walking along their banks was rarely possible in the past. Now the banks have been opened up and public pathways and local people are encouraged to walk there. In short it's better! (Pauline Tambling)

This optimistic note is one ending to Pauline's memoir; another heading, which she never developed, and which so far as I could see, was what she was going to write next, was called 'Swimming and Angel Drove', which was about the primitive conditions in which she learned to swim (she was an enthusiastic swimmer, and a good one). It is all I have been able to rescue from fragments which she never quite completed, or got into an order which she was happy with. I emailed her then closest friend, Rosemary and got this answer:

Hi Jeremy, I have just googled Angel Grove as I couldn't quite remember the name of the lane, as it was then, where the pool was. It was an open air swimming pool with the usual wooden changing cubicles on either side of the pool, 3 diving boards at one end and some large steps at the other end, covered in grey paving slabs, deep enough for people to sit on in a tiered effect. It wasn't heated and very cold, especially at the beginning of the season. The temperature was always shown on a small blackboard at the entrance. I remember it was quite often 58 degrees. The pool was really the most exciting activity you could do in Ely!

So again, we have the contrast, between the dull conditions she speaks of in childhood and the career she went on to have, starting as a lively classroom teacher (a little before her death she had an email from one pupil she taught back in the late 1970s); and the Education Officer she became at the Royal Opera House, where comedy and chaos and deep inefficiency and contention raged. In bringing this Memoir to a close, I want to mention some other names as an acknowledgement of all she was able to accomplish. I begin with Sally Bacon's speech about her at the commemorative event held at the Round House:

I first met Pauline more than 30 years ago when we were both based in Covent Garden, she at the Opera House and me working in my first proper job as Education Officer at the Poetry Society just up the road from her. Drawn together by proximity, we hit it off and were starting to develop a project focused on libretti, but I moved on to work on children's programmes at the National Trust and for a while we weren't working together directly. Meanwhile Opera House projects at various National Trust properties continued to develop during this time as the head of the Trust was also Chair of the Royal Opera House, and so, as Pauline liked to say, our orbits continued to align!

In 1997 I moved on to run a grant-making foundation supporting the arts and education, and when Pauline arrived at the Arts Council soon after (in the first of her five senior roles there), I was straight through her door in her very first week to discuss the possibility of creating a National Children's Art Awards scheme. Within minutes she'd had the idea of a National Children's Art Day, which we proceeded to fund as part of the Art Awards, and this still exists, under a different name and with a different funder, today. Such was Pauline's genius – in five minutes she could have ideas that weren't even anything to do with her day job but they still took flight and pretty soon no one involved even had the least clue they originated with her!

Having worked in arts learning, we were both now funders – public and private – and could collaborate more closely, and again, Pauline was the first person I talked to when my foundation wanted to do something about leadership training in the arts sector. When we put together what we very grandly called a task force to work on this, our museums colleague quickly fell away and basically it was just Pauline and me, working closely with John Holden, who is here today, and Robert Hewison to put together a programme to address the leadership development needs of a sector which was investing very little in training. She was a key eminence grise throughout the process of developing the Clore Leadership programme, long before the Clore Duffield board agreed to fund it. For those of you who don't know it, the programme trains leaders in the cultural sector. Pauline helped us to interview and appoint Chris Smith as the programme's first director, and joined the founding board alongside the directors of the National Theatre, the Royal Opera House and Tate, and remained a trustee until 2017 – of course it's entirely against best practice to have someone on a board for so long, but we just couldn't let her go – until, sadly, her diagnosis in 2017, when she finally stood down. This year Clore Leadership celebrates its 20th anniversary and has now trained more than two and a half thousand leaders, plenty of whom are here today. I love that Pauline's fingerprints were all over its creation and early success, and she had a key role for more than a decade and a half. It was just one of so many things that she either steered or created. She made an incredible array of programmes, initiatives and opportunities happen. She was the prime mover behind Creative Partnerships and Youth Music – so many things existed, or still exist, because of Pauline. The same applied when we set up the Cultural Learning Alliance to champion a right to arts and culture for every child. My first conversation about doing this was with Pauline. She sat on the project's first strategy group which led to the creation of the Alliance, then joined its first Steering Board, then sat on its Advisory Panel. Our fabulous Trustee, Tina Ramdeen, who works here, came to us via Pauline. She was invaluable in all her various roles with us for a decade and a half.

When Pauline left her role as CEO of CCSkills (the Skills Council for arts and culture) in 2017, after a decade leading the cultural skills agenda, their loss was the wider arts sector's gain. She proceeded to take on many non-executive roles, write articles and comment pieces, and do much informal mentoring. For me, Pauline's freedom from a day job meant regular breakfast catch-ups, usually at Bill's Café in Victoria, where we sat for much longer than intended, setting the world to rights over pancakes and blueberries. After a quick catch up on family, these meetings generally focused on arts learning, leadership, and, of course, laughter. I always left inspired and with a plan to navigate a particular thorny issue or full of new ideas.

At the close of 2021 she had the brilliant idea – Pauline always had such brilliant ideas – of revisiting the seminal 1982 Gulbenkian The Arts in Schools report 40 years after, and which had led to the creation of her own education role at the Royal Opera House. Finally we were able to work together properly with a single shared purpose and it took her career right back to where it had begun. Gulbenkian provided the funding for a new version, in partnership with A New Direction, so we could work with our wonderful colleague Steve Moffit, its CEO, who had known Pauline for as long as I had. It was the perfect project for her: Pauline's knowledge across the 40 year-period and across the arts, education, training and skills was second to none. She still had a much-thumbed and heavily annotated copy of the original 1982 report to hand – although I think it was actually handed on to her by Kate who is speaking next!

Neither of us had fully anticipated the scale of the task – it was a huge piece of work, but we loved it. We complemented each other perfectly. Pauline was performing arts; I was literature and visual arts. Pauline (quite rightly) couldn't care less about a misplaced comma – I would lose sleep over it! We managed all the thinking and writing collaboratively through endless long phone calls and emails, and Pauline brought all her brilliance, wisdom and clarity – and her contacts – to the process. The most difficult task was wrestling all our many findings into 10 clear recommendations for the sector and for the next government. It was her last big project, and we were so grateful that she could finish it, and that she stayed well enough to speak at the report's launch in March. As Steve Moffitt said to me the other day, the report was Pauline's final gift to us all. Now those of us in the arts education world need to use it, work with it and realise the many ideas and solutions within it.

Throughout all my work with her, family life was never far away. It was in the ping of an oven timer when we were on a call as she had to take out a cake she had baked; it was in the days allocated to looking after her three adored grandchildren when I knew better than to try and reach her; it was in the stories of her eldest granddaughter's early years education (it was of course impossible to disconnect that from her scrutiny of education policy!); it was evident in her huge pride in Kirsten and Felix and her pleasure in Suffolk weekends and trips or outings with Jeremy. Her family was her absolute bedrock and her commitment to her work never removed her focus from that.

Sometimes her domestic and professional lives would bleed into each other – the design of her kitchen shelves in Suffolk (which many of you will have seen on Zoom calls, or in real life) were a homage to her multi-award winning Backstage Centre in Thurrock. She loved those shelves and was cross when an estate agent recently failed to note their quality or care about their special provenance, and omitted them from all the photographs he took. I am so glad we got to visit Pauline and Jeremy there last year and of course she had baked a cake. Pauline always knew exactly how to mark an occasion – usually with champagne.

I've obviously been thinking a lot about Pauline's brilliance recently. Steve Moffitt wrote when she died that she was 'a great boss, a fabulous collaborator and an exceptional thinker and strategist.' She was also a close and loyal friend to us both. In his blog about her in December Steve described Pauline as a powerhouse, a dynamo of ideas and energy – the queen of finding solutions, and he is exactly right. No one was better at working through a problem. She was so generous with her time, with listening to the problems of others, as well as being so practical and fabulous at just making things happen. She had a unique ability to apply a wide angle lens to any situation when the rest of us were still down in the long weeds. She was a warm, generous guiding light for so many people. She was always making connections and offering encouragement. To quote Steve again – sorry Steve! – 'Pauline was not only a wonderful leader ... but she was also an exceptional human being.'

A close friend who's here today once said that if you've worked for big organisations in the cultural sector then you are skilled at dealing with adversity and caprice. Pauline always found things to laugh about in the difficulties she encountered, and the difficult people she and I worked with along the way. We shared the ability to take the horror stories and turn them into amusing anecdotes, if only just for each other. I realise now that it was a brilliantly effective strategy for navigating difficulty.

She was very active on Twitter until the middle of last year, and took on all the social media communications for the Arts in Schools report, going down quite a rabbit hole by following many, many school leaders, teachers and education commentators. When she came off Twitter in the middle of last year I really missed her presence there. It signalled a stepping away from engagement which was a marker of things to come. She was working until the end, on a history of the learning and participation programme at the Royal Opera House and interviewing people from her past, so again her life was coming full circle. There was such a circularity to the arc of her career, and of course CC Skills announced its closure shortly before we lost Pauline. She completed articles about this in her final days —she sent me her last piece to finish after she'd dictated it to Felix: 'cut what you like' she said, 'I trust you completely'. It was typical of Pauline that she reflected on the organisation's past achievements, but absolutely pulled no punches in her clear-sightedness about what more needs to be done. Pauline had a rare ability to see the connection between the arts aspiration and opportunities children are given in school, their access to opportunities in work, and the policy structures needed to make these happen. No one understood this better.

We were due to have lunch on the 6th of December (2023). In the end it was one of life's great ironies that someone so unstintingly clearsighted had her vision compromised by the spread of her cancer. When it became hard for her to see, it was clear that time was running out. As she said occasionally during her years of monthly newly developed 'infusions' as she called them, 'one day my luck will run out'. We often talked about her illness and the treatments involved. She felt that in spite of all the challenges in our health system, there was always a little corner of the NHS where a red carpet was rolled out for her — at St George's, Tooting, and then at Barts, just round the corner from the flat in the Barbican— and for this she was grateful.

> *Picasso once wrote to Matisse, "We must talk to each other as much as we can. When one of us dies, there will be some things that the other will never be able to talk of with anyone else." I know I'm not the only one here who will feel that way about Pauline. I've realised since her death just how many of those things we talked about were laughter-inducing – things that would tickle her that would mystify most other people. And, like many of us, I was just so used to being able to ask for her bloody brilliant advice. Now we will only be able to imagine what she might say to us. For those of us who worked closely with her I hope she will remain a voice at our shoulders in all that we do, and that she will continue to sharpen our work and to make it better. Weren't we all so very, very lucky to have known her.*

I must supplement Sally Bacon's account with an email from Steve Moffitt, telling me: 'I first met Pauline in 1996. When I started ENO. She was my equivalent but at the ROH. She just had more experience and was able to talk about Opera Education in a much more articulate way than I was able to. I remember she was instrumental in setting up RESEO the European Opera Education network. I think that's when I met her first in November/December when she set it up. I remember she shuffled over to me in Stuttgart at the second continental gathering that we had there in the following year and said to me "We should get to know each other. I think you might be surprised at what we have in common". She then left for the Arts Council to lead their National Education team. Whilst I was at ENO we didn't collaborate or work together. I just attended lots of meetings with her in her new role. It was when I was at Creative Partnerships that we made stuff happen ... Pauline was always drawing diagrams and modelling programmes. I did see her when she was at CC Skills. The biggest thing we did together was something like the Future Jobs fund – I can't remember what it was called – but we created 100 jobs for kids!

Pauline's heart was in the Opera House, under Sir John Tolley, and Jeremy Isaacs, and sundry others. Funding, as said, came partly from the Gulbenkian Foundation, which, under Peter Brinson's leadership, played a major role in developing the role of the artist in society – for details, see *Experience and Experiment: The UK Branch of the Calouste Gulbenkian Foundation 1956-2006* by Robert Hewison and John Holden (2006). There was a growing realisation that if the arts were to thrive there needed to be engagement between schools, communities and the professional arts. The Arts Council of Great Britain started to encourage its funded organisations to set up education departments. I have been reminded of how much Pauline enjoyed her time at ROH by Kate Castle, her opposite number in Ballet Education. Kate was trained at the Royal Ballet School, and danced with the Royal Ballet at ROH, as well as in film and television, but retrained as a primary school teacher, and was one of the first dance animateurs, funded by Greater London Arts, working with schools and communities in East London.

I follow up Sally Bacon's tribute with that given on the same occasion by Kate Castle:

I'd like to begin by thanking Jeremy, Kirsten and Felix for inviting me to share my memories of Pauline with you all today. It's a huge honour, but also a huge responsibility: to be entrusted with sharing with you all glimpses of the Pauline that I knew and had grown to love. It's especially difficult because she was such a multi-faceted personality with achievements in so many different areas of her life. It always seemed to me as if she had 48 hours in her day to everyone else's 24. She just got so much done.

Even though I knew she was living with cancer, I must confess that her death – as it so often does – caught me by surprise. She was seemingly still so vibrant, busy and active until the final days, so that it seemed she just slipped away almost without my noticing. But perhaps that was what she wanted – still to be active in the world, writing a passionately eloquent article for Arts Professional, and to then, suddenly be no longer with us.

But I have also realized that with typical foresight she had in fact been preparing for the end for several years and working diligently on her legacy. For example, she had been working through lockdown [2020-2021] on an account of her family history, and in 2022 she invited me to take part in a series of conversations which would document the history of the education programme at the Royal Opera House, our working relationship and implicitly our friendship. A mutually agreed version of this document is now lodged in the Opera House archive. It's fitting that a journey that began with the Gulbenkian Arts in Schools report in 1982 should end with the review of this seminal publication in 2023 in which Pauline played such a key and driving role.

It is absolutely true to state that Pauline's professional life embodies the history of the development of artists and cultural organisations working in collaboration with schools and the community to increase engagement – a cause she was fighting for until the very end.

I'm now going to draw now upon Pauline's own words. Her story shows how her own childhood experience of the arts led to a lifelong commitment. "A second-hand piano proved to be my passport to the arts. My father worked as a labourer for a builder in Ely, where we lived and one day, he was helping to strip out an old house, when the owner offered the piano to the workers. I was probably about seven or eight – and wanted to learn to play. My mother signed me up for weekly lessons with a local piano teacher. My primary education was at an old-fashioned Church of England school. Our arts lessons were live BBC Radio broadcasts: Time and Tune, Singing Together *and* Music and Movement. *At Grammar School we had free access to the loan of an instrument and to weekly group lessons. I took up the clarinet. The school had chamber groups, choirs and an orchestra, and there were Saturday classes and a County Youth Orchestra in Cambridge. We had art lessons and the teachers always had their own work on the go in the corner of the art room which was inspiring because the idea that an adult might paint for pleasure was new to most of us. I have three memories of professional arts activity in my school years: a touring production of* Waiting for Godot *in our school hall, a trip to the RSC for Peter Brook's* A Midsummer Night's Dream *and a production of* Othello *at the Mermaid. Those few professional productions made a huge impact on me. During our first year in the sixth form we all did work experience. I was allocated to an infant school a few yards from my school. This was an enlightened institution full of colour and play. I applied for teacher training and started a three-year Certificate of Education course and in 1978 replied to an advert for a 'piano-playing class teacher' at a one-form entry primary school in rural Essex. I had to accompany hymns at daily assembly, lead hymn practice weekly, organise choir, recorder and guitar clubs, co-produce the annual school productions and ensure the school did well at county choir and music festivals. I had no qualifications for running these activities but Essex County Council organised teacher training sessions for music staff [Pauline had singing lessons and guitar-playing lessons – Jeremy Tambling]. The prospect of getting a Deputy Headship in my late twenties made me question my future career. I applied for two jobs: one to run a film project at the Ipswich Arts Cinema and the other as Education Officer for the Royal Opera.*

This account of her early experiences will illuminate how she came to become such a powerful advocate for young people's engagement with the arts and culture. It also shows just how much has been lost in present-day education.

I first met Pauline 40 years ago in 1983 when she came to interview for that post. I'd been appointed Education Officer in 1982 to work for the Royal Ballet and Sadler's Wells Royal Ballet – as it was then – moving offices four times until we finally seemed to have arrived and were settled next to Sir John Tooley's office with a full-time administrator. You know when you meet someone for the first time and you just know? My first impressions of Pauline were of someone with an enormous and authentic inner confidence, an air of serenity and calm and potentially, a playful streak. She had not one iota of arrogance, but you just knew she would get the job done. We got on from the start and it's fair to say our working relationship was based on mutual respect, liking and a shared sense of humour about the at times absurd situations we found ourselves in. In those early days we laughed loudly and often at the privilege, pomposity and patriarchy which occasionally frustrated our ambitions: to share the richness of opera and ballet and the resources of the ROH with the wider world. Pauline always managed to be both respectful and iconoclastic in her wish make the joy of opera and culture in general for the many not the few.

She approached the task in her characteristic manner – through calm and careful planning, diplomacy in all her encounters, and above all in making lifelong partnerships. For example, she paired with the Metropolitan Opera in New York in bringing the 'Write an Opera' model, which is still running. We collaborated on week-long enrichment courses for sixth-formers and Insight days for audiences. We caused chaos with Family Fun Days in the Crush Bar and delivered six schools' matinees a year for ballet and opera with a wrap-around programme of talks, resource materials and INSET days.

It's also worth noting that both Pauline and I became mothers while we were working at The Royal Opera House and this in itself was groundbreaking. I remember a conversation we had at the Stage Door with an eminent female Board member who said 'I don't know what's the matter with you girls. You have perfectly good jobs and then you go wanting children as well.' I leave you to imagine the reply.

So – lots of fun, yes, partly because this evolving world of professional artists working in education and the community was new to everyone. We were essentially making it up as we went along, although we had terrific support from teachers, education advisers, and the participants themselves. On encountering us one day Sir John Tooley said: "What are you two up to now?" – and we looked at each other and said: "Mischief!". It was exhilarating and stimulating and a good foundation for a lifelong friendship, sustained in part by the support we gave each other as parents in a world which was not always sympathetic to those needs.

Losing Pauline has made me think about what true friendship entails. For me - Pauline was totally trust-worthy, loyal and always had my best interests at heart. There was no subject off limits. And as you've probably gathered by now, we laughed a lot. Our last communication was a sharing of amusing anecdotes about our grandchildren. And anyone who visited Pauline will know how one was warmly welcomed, settled with a glass of wine before enjoying a fabulous meal – for Pauline was a great cook. But she was always modest about her accomplishments – being a dexterous quilter was one of them and she produced some beautifully crafted pieces. A metaphor perhaps for the way she carefully pieced and stitched together the various elements of her life.

Her marriage to Jeremy was a true partnership with each supporting the other in their respective careers. Above all she was a wonderful mother and grandmother who absolutely adored her three grandchildren: Frances, Emil and Sidonie.

I've always thought that the world was held together not just by the grand gestures but by a million small acts of kindness. It's the web that binds us to each other. Pauline was one of the kindest people I have ever known. You parted with either a consoling hand, a new contact, a reading suggestion, or a fresh perspective on a problem. Every encounter with her left one feeling better somehow – a better version of oneself.

Pauline's professional legacy is assured – she was a fierce warrior in the battle for equity and opportunity – but what will also be missed is her immense intelligence, humanity and above all kindness, for which all that is left to be said is – thank you for everything – from us all.

Pauline worked with many singers: Elizabeth Bainbridge, and John Dobson stand out, as does the conductor Edward Lambert, and Davis Syrus, the *repetiteur* and Wagnerian; and the archivist at the ROH, Francesca Franchi; and Tess Forsey; and among volunteers, Rozzie Metherell. Kate Castle and Pauline set up an Education Committee - members included John Stephens, Inspector, ILEA (Inner-London Education Authority), who was a key advisor to Pauline, as he chaired her Education Committee at the ROH. His work was very helpful. Another was Michael Marland, then head of North Westminster Community School, well known for his commitment to the arts in schools. The purpose of creating an advisory group for Ballet Education and then a combined Education Committee with representation on the Board of ROH plc was firstly to offer credibility by stacking it with outsiders but people who were highly respected; people such as Professors Joan White and June Layson, James Porter, Director of The Commonwealth Institute, and Jill Henderson who was the senior PE adviser for ILEA and a dance specialist. The hope was that they would offer deep knowledge about and understanding of the developing relationship between the arts in schools and the curriculum and artists working in schools, and that they would act as ambassadors and advocates for the work, by opening doors externally and softening hardened attitudes within. They would offer a view of the wider world, challenging 'group think' and 'founder syndrome' – which occurs when the pioneering founder hangs onto the ball and doesn't give other players a chance. Pauline never departed from that. Her role at the Arts Council of England was very senior, immediately under Peter Hewitt the then CEO, in an organisation whose decline and present management, which Pauline felt had affected the BBC, especially Radio 3, she regarded as symptomatic of a government revenge against the enlightening possibilities of the creative arts in education. Her work was exemplary, even when she was having chemotherapy in 2003-204. She criss-crossed England: one day she was in Birmingham (starting from London) in the morning and Cambridge in the afternoon, I remember. Her work for Creative and Cultural Skills, and her desire to create apprenticeships for students who wanted to work backstage was truly dynamic, though it was also frustrated by funding which was not as protected as that of the Royal Opera House. But that very niche context for her work she had definitely outgrown, and her interest was, finally, in opening up educational opportunities for young people. Marcus Davey reminds me in an email:

> *Pauline was a Trustee of the Roundhouse Trust, Chair of the Campus Committee (overseeing the construction of Roundhouse Works building), Chair of the Evaluation Committee and a member of the Business, Audit and Risk Committee (overseeing our financial operations, commercial activity and H&S audit and culture). Yes, she was incredibly involved and wonderfully committed, although looking back I think we may have taken advantage of her incredible skills and experience… but she enabled us to be the organisation we are today. We named the room after her in Roundhouse Works because she worked so hard to oversee the development and construction of the building. It is a permanent reminder to us all of her deep commitment and passion for the Roundhouse and our work with young people.*

And that was Pauline, as well as an exceptional wife and mother, and someone who loved opera, and who in her last years became a formidable pianist - her teacher, Julian Larkin, a church organist and performer lived in Saxmundham, not far from Woodbridge. (Our cottage in Woodbridge had an exceptional garden, I will add, which was Pauline's sole creation.) Julian thought she was a crypto-Grade 8 student who didn't want to acknowledge it. On the piano, she played Bach, and Schubert, the latter her favourite; that was the music, apart from opera, which she always listened to. Julian attended the commemoration for her at the Roundhouse, with his wife and stepson.

To all who helped Pauline, and worked with her, and loved her, and have helped to bring this Memoir to light, my thanks.

Bibliography

Ashton, Patrick. *Preserving Ely: The Story of Ely Jam Factory*. The Ely Society, 2013.

Austin, Matthew D. *The Buildings of Tower Hospital, Ely: A Photographic Portrait*. Matthew D. Austin, 2015.

Barrowclough, David, and Morrison, Kate. *Ely: The Hidden History*. Stroud, Gloucestershire: The History Press, 2013.

Bentham, James. *The History and Antiquities of the Conventual and Cathedral Church of Ely: from the foundation of the monastery, A.D. 673. To the year 1771*. Cambridge: Cambridge University Press, 1771. 2 vols.

Clements, J.H. *A Brief History of Ely and Neighbouring Villages in the Isle*. Ely: Clements and Sons, 1868.

Darby, H. C. *The Changing Fenland*. Cambridge: Cambridge University Press, 1983.

— *The Draining of the Fens*. Cambridge, Cambridge University Press, 1956.

— *The Medieval Fenland*. Cambridge: Cambridge University Press, 1940

Denton, Audrey. *Waterside, Ely: Yesterday and Today*. Bottisham, Cambridgeshire: The Granta Press, 1983.

Dorman, Bernard E. *The Story of Ely and its Cathedral*. Norwich: Black Horse, 1986.

Gill, E. R. *Recollections of Littleport*. Wisbech, Cambridgeshire: Charles N. Veal & Company, [undated].

Franklin, William: *An Agricultural History of Ely*. Ely History Publications, 2017.

— *The Hospital of St John and St Mary Magdalene in Ely, and its successor, St John's Farm*. Ely History Publications, 2018.

Hall, Shirley. *Holy Trinity Ely 1566-1938: Church and Parish*. Shirley Hall, 2022.

Harlock, Alva S. *Bygone Littleport: A Collection of Sketches*. St. George's Church Parish Magazine, Littleport, 1975.

Liber Eliensis: A History of the Isle of Ely From the Seventh Century to the Twelfth. Translated by Janet Fairweather. Woodbridge: The Boydell Press, 2005.

Meeres, Frank. *The Story of the Fens*. Stroud, Gloucestershire: The History Press, 2019.

Rotherham, Ian D. *The Lost Fens: England's Greatest Ecological Disaster*. Stroud, Gloucestershire: The History Press, 2013.

Rouse, Mike, and Holmes, Reg. *Ely, Cathedral City and Market Town: The Second in a Series of Pictorial Records 1900-1953*. Ely: The Ely Society, 1975.

Scharfe, Norman. *Cambridgeshire: A Shell Guide*. London; Faber and Faber, 1983.

Venneberg, Paul, et al. *Buck's Grove United Methodist Church Centennial: 1879 to 1979*. 1979.

This book is printed on paper from sustainable sources managed under the Forest Stewardship Council (FSC) scheme.

It has been printed in the UK to reduce transportation miles and their impact upon the environment.

For every new title that Troubador publishes, we plant a tree to offset CO_2, partnering with the More Trees scheme.

For more about how Troubador offsets its environmental impact, see www.troubador.co.uk/sustainability-and-community

This book is printed on paper from sustainable sources managed under the Forest Stewardship Council (FSC) scheme.

It has been printed in the UK to reduce transportation miles and their impact upon the environment.

For every new title that Troubador publishes, we plant a tree to offset CO_2, partnering with the More Trees scheme.

For more about how Troubador offsets its environmental impact, see www.troubador.co.uk/sustainability-and-community